The Internet
Instant Reference
Third Edition

Paul E. Hoffman

SYBEX®

San Francisco • Paris • Düsseldorf • Soest

Associate Publisher: Carrie Lavine
Acquisitions Manager: Kristine Plachy
Developmental Editor: Dan Brodnitz
Editor: Suzanne Rotondo
Technical Editor: Michelle Moore
Book Designer: Ingrid Owen
Technical Art: Cuong Le
Desktop Publisher: Deborah A. Bevilacqua
Production Coordinator: Kim Askew-Qasem
Editorial Assistant: Heather O'Connor
Cover Designer: Design Site

Table of Contents

Part 2

Using the Internet

25

Index

315

Introduction

Welcome to the *Internet Instant Reference*, the complete pocket reference to the huge and complex world of the Internet. This book tells you everything you need to know to use the Internet, and it does so in a way that makes it easy to find what you need quickly.

WHAT IS THE INTERNET?

Describing the Internet is like describing a city: you can talk about the landscape, the streets, the stores, the government, the people, the weather, or a combination of all of them—there are many parts that make up the whole. The Internet is confusing for many computer users because it is different from anything they are used to. It's not a program, it's not a piece of hardware, it's not software, it's not even a system. Instead, it is a place where you can get information, make information available (for free or for sale), and where you can meet people.

Essentially, the Internet is a network of computers that offer access to people and information. Over 40 million people use the Internet, and that number is expected to increase to over 100 million within a few years. To use the Internet, you run many different programs depending on the type of information you wish to view. For example, you might use one program for mail, another program for retrieving files, and yet a third for playing fantasy games with many people at once. The kind of information freely available includes government documents, scientific data, hobbyist lists, business and personal advertising, databases, and much more.

When you speak of "the Internet," then, you can think of it as a combination of the network, the people who use it, all of the programs used to get information, and the information itself. People from all over the world can access the Internet, and more than 10 million do so daily. Most of these people only use one feature of the Internet—mail—but many also use additional features. (This book uses the term *mail* for what many call *electronic mail* or *email* because all mail on the Internet is electronic. On the Internet, paper-based mail is often jokingly called *snailmail* to contrast it with instantaneous Internet mail.)

WHO USES THE INTERNET?

Even though the Internet is nebulous and difficult to define, its value is easy to see. If you are "on" the Internet, meaning you have regular access to it, you can communicate with anyone else on the Internet quickly and easily. Almost anything you can do through the regular mail system or on the telephone can also be done on the Internet.

The kinds of communication that happen on the Internet every day include the following:

- exchanging short social notes
- getting the latest news from around the world
- conducting business negotiations
- collaborating on scientific research
- exchanging information with others who have similar hobbies or interests
- transferring computer files

As you can imagine, with such a wide range of types of communications, the range of people who use the Internet is also diverse. Some corporations use the Internet for all of their important in-company communications; many also provide information to their customers on the Internet. An increasing number of U.S. and state government agencies are publishing general information on the Internet. Almost every major university in the country (and many outside the U.S.) use the Internet for academic communications.

Besides the business and educational uses of the Internet, there are many exciting features for the individual user. Millions of people use the Internet only for social and general-interest purposes. The entertainment interest groups are usually the most active, and they generate much more interest than the interest groups related strictly to business.

The Internet is open to anyone who can use a computer and a modem and can call into a computer that is on the Internet. At many universities and companies, the entire network at the location is connected to the Internet. Most people, however, access the Internet from their own computers through modems.

ABOUT THIS BOOK

Even though the Internet is a gigantic place with lots of nooks and crannies, a small book such as this can give you a complete reference on how to use the programs and where to start looking for information. This book is designed for all levels of Internet users, from complete beginners to advanced users, to give you enough of what you need to go out on your own.

Because of the Internet's unusual organization, it is impossible to describe it in a hierarchical order. Therefore, the major part of the book is an alphabetical list of topics that cover the many different programs, concepts, organizations, and terms you might encounter on the Internet.

The Internet can be divided into two levels: the user's arena and the technical arena. The technical arena includes the communications protocols used between computers on the Internet, the structure of the communications systems, the connection mechanisms, and so on. As a user, you may come across these terms occasionally, but most users never need to know about this level of technical detail. These topics are only touched on in this book.

Searching for information on the Internet is an art that could never be covered completely, but with a few dozen tools of the trade, you will be equipped to start searching on your own. All of the tools you need to know are covered thoroughly here. You won't find listings of all of the possible places to look for things, because such a list is always out-of-date and incomplete; instead, you'll find a complete guide to good starting points for your search.

WHAT YOU'LL FIND INSIDE

This book has two main parts:

- Part 1 introduces the Internet, tells you how to get on the Internet if you are not already there, describes the tools you will be using, and discusses the major attributes of the Internet. Even if you have already accessed some Internet resources before, you should read this part to get a better understanding of the depth and breadth of the Internet.

- Part 2 is the main reference. It is organized alphabetically by topic, with plenty of cross-references so that you can find what you need quickly. Some entries describe programs you use while on the Internet, some describe important terms, and some describe the groups of people that have the most influence on the way the Internet works. You can read just the topics you are interested in, or read it from A to Z to get a complete overview of what the Internet is all about.

Of course, there is also a complete index to help you find specific information instantly.

HOW TO FIND INFORMATION

Many of the sections in Part 2 tell you how to get specific information from the Internet. These look like the section below.

FOR MORE INFORMATION

Service:	**Gopher**
Host:	`fatty.law.cornell.edu`
Path:	*whole server*
Description:	A great deal of legal information from the Cornell Law School. It contains lots of reference information, legal codes, federal rules, and so on.

This example tells you how to get legal information from a computer at Cornell Law School using the Gopher service.

Each of the services shown in the For More Information sections
are described in Part 1. They are also discussed in full detail
throughout Part 2.

HOW TO GIVE COMMANDS

Many of the entries in Part 2 refer you to sources of information on
the Internet. Reaching those sources may require you to use different Internet programs. Those programs are discussed in Part 1.

There are many ways to access the Internet. A few years ago, most
Internet users came in through Unix computers. Now, most people
in the U.S. use graphical programs like Netscape on their personal
computers. This book covers both kinds of programs.

Because many computers on the Internet use Unix as an operating
system, Part 1 also has a brief guide to the most common Unix commands that you might use. Unix commands are shown in **boldface**

characters. On most Unix systems, you type a command name after a prompt, as described in Part 1. In this book, Unix commands are shown after a prompt that is not in boldface:

```
% gopher
```

Here, the command you type is **gopher,** and the % is the Unix prompt that is already on the screen. Mail addresses are listed in program font.

THE INTERNET AWAITS YOU

Regardless of how you read this book, you will probably find that it takes you deeper into the Internet than you have ever been. Keep this book at your side to help you face the techno-babble and the confusion fully armed. Most important, be sure to have fun as you explore the Internet!

Part 1

Internet Overview

Using the Internet is like touring a large wildlife reserve: there are many things you never dreamed of (some of them wild, some of them tame); getting from one point to another can be done using very different kinds of vehicles; many so-called experts don't know enough to help you in a sticky situation; you're not sure if you will have enough film to record everything you see; and no one who hasn't been there will believe your stories when you get home.

The Internet is constantly growing, and there is always room for more people. The technical foundation of the Internet allows it to keep expanding almost infinitely without bogging down or filling up. (Like other dreams, this might turn out to be false ten years from now when there are hundreds of millions or billions of people on the Internet, but it is nice to dream for now.)

HISTORY OF THE INTERNET

You may wonder how something as flexible and expandable as the Internet came to exist. Its history is interesting: little from the first 20 years of its existence has much resemblance to its current or future uses. The Internet was originally a military project used only for defense purposes. It then became a link for academic institutions sharing research results, and then evolved into a medium for mixed academic, commercial, and personal uses. It is still growing and changing, and there is no way to predict what it will turn into in the next five or ten years.

BEFORE THE BEGINNING

In the mid-1960s, computer networking was in its infancy. Few of the existing computers could communicate at anywhere near the speed at which they could process data. The most common form of communication between two computers was manual: Computer A would write out a magnetic tape or a stack of punched cards, a human would take the tape or cards from Computer A and move them to Computer B, and Computer B would read the data. For Computer A to communicate with many other computers, the process would have to be repeated for each machine.

More advanced computer communications networks had been developed, but they were crude in comparison to today's computers. A network of three or more computers could be wired together and could communicate at low speeds, but a constant problem with early communications was that each computer had to be functioning for the network to function. Thus, if one computer was turned off for maintenance, the network would not function unless the computer was removed from the network. This made networking unreliable and difficult to manage.

THE ADVENT OF ARPANET

The U.S. Department of Defense was an early supporter of much of the research into advanced computers and networking. Even in the mid-1960s, the U.S. military relied on computer technology, so advances in that area were of critical importance. A network that could be shut down by a single computer's malfunction was a major vulnerability, so the military wanted to develop a network that could survive even if one or many of the computers on the network didn't.

Around 1970, the Advanced Research Projects Agency, part of the Department of Defense, set up the first parts of what would become the Internet. There were many goals for this network, dubbed the *ARPAnet*, all of which were implemented and are still a part of today's Internet. Some of those goals included the following:

- The network would be able to run even if many of the computers or the connections between them failed.

- To accommodate the many different types of computers coming onto the market, the Defense Department wanted dissimilar computers to be able to exchange information smoothly. Thus, the networking method had to be usable by computers with vastly different hardware configurations.

- The network would be capable of automatically rerouting information around non-functioning parts of the network. To compare this with a road trip, imagine you are driving on the interstate from New York to Boston. If your planned route through Hartford was blocked by an accident, you could take the highway through Providence instead. If both those routes were unavailable, you could take a third route through Albany. The network had to be capable of this sort of automatic rerouting.

- The ARPAnet was to be a network of networks, not just a network of computers. Only one computer on a network had to be connected directly to the ARPAnet hardware. Every other computer on that local network would appear to be "on" the ARPAnet and could communicate with other computers on the ARPAnet through the one connection.

The ARPAnet expanded to non-military uses in the 1970s, when universities and companies doing defense-related research were allowed to use the network. This increased use allowed the researchers who maintained the ARPAnet to study how growth in the number of computers and users changed the way the ARPAnet responded. It also gave researchers a glimpse of what the potential difficulties in running the network would be. For example, while many had assumed the hardest thing would be maintaining the speed of the network, keeping every computer speaking the same language was more of a challenge.

In the late 1970s, the ARPAnet was so large that the original standards would not support the rate of growth of the network. After years of research (and a fair amount of arguing), the ARPAnet switched from a technology known as Package Switch Nodes to the *TCP/IP* communication standard. TCP/IP is a communication protocol that defines how to send particular kinds of messages between different computers. The biggest advantage of TCP/IP was that it allowed for almost unlimited growth in the size of the network and was easily implemented on a variety of computer hardware. By 1983, all computers on the ARPAnet were required to use TCP/IP.

If researchers had not set down these standards, the ARPAnet would have never gotten off the ground. Once the standards were set, the ARPAnet flourished. It was used mostly with non-defense applications. People wrote programs that allowed easier access to files on other computers, then programs that facilitated cooperative communication between computers on the ARPAnet. Companies and universities all over the world got connected to the Internet, and many foreign governments supported connections so that their researchers could communicate with colleagues in the U.S.

NSFNET

Because it was clear that much of the ARPAnet was being used for non-military purposes, the Department of Defense created a military-only network called MILNET. A few years later, the National Science Foundation used the model of the ARPAnet to form the *NSFnet*, which linked together NSF researchers. Most colleges and companies who were on the NSFnet were also on the ARPAnet, and the two networks used the same communications links (TCP/IP), so the two systems began to combine and cooperate. The NSF began funding higher-speed links for the NSFnet, and also supported the same kind of network research that had moved the ARPAnet forward in its early years. The Department of Defense did not maintain the ARPAnet at the same level the NSF did the

NSFnet, and by the late 1980s, the ARPAnet faded away and was absorbed by the NSFnet.

Around 1980, two unaffiliated networks started up. Usenet and BITNET were grass-roots networks based on the concepts of free access to information and ease of use. These two networks were unaffiliated with the ARPAnet, but as the ARPAnet grew, users wanted to share information across networks. Thus, connections were built between the networks so that mail and news could be connected. Other new commercial networks such as CompuServe and America Online also drew large constituencies, and many people found themselves on more than one network.

The Internet, then, is an amalgam of many networks that participate to a larger or smaller extent. The term "Internet" with a capital *I* became the de facto name for the network in the late 1980s, but there is no specific thing you can call "the Internet."

THE INTERNET TODAY AND TOMORROW

Recently, everyone has wanted to get in on the Internet. A widely talked-about idea a few years ago was the National Research and Education Network (NREN). The NREN, which was sponsored by Al Gore when he was a senator, would give Internet access to virtually all kindergarten, elementary, and high school students, and give better access to non-research colleges and universities. The idea was to give the American education system the same communication tools that were already being used by the government, military, and private businesses. Teachers could share teaching ideas, students could do cooperative projects, and everyone would get a taste of what was happening in the world of computing other than video games.

Another major movement on the Internet is toward open commercial use. The Commercial Internet Exchange (CIX), a group of companies that provides private access to the Internet, is now one of several organizations formed for this purpose. For decades, many people who had no real connection with the Department of Defense or the NSF got accounts on Internet machines illegally. Without many of these people, the Internet wouldn't be what it is today. When the existence of these non-affiliated users was finally acknowledged, it was clear that some means of access should be provided above-board. The NSF started letting commercial providers give access to the Internet, on the condition that those commercial providers paid their fair share (what a "fair share" is has never been clearly defined).

Today, if you have a modem, you can get on the Internet for free. If you want more reliability, you can sign on with one of the commercial providers for a small amount of money. Appendix A lists many service providers that will let you set up an account so that you can access the Internet any time you want. If you are at a university or company that already has Internet access, your system administrator can probably get you on the Internet within hours.

The future of the Internet is impossible to predict. Clearly, the number of people with Internet access will continue to grow. President Clinton's National Information Infrastructure (NII) proposal for expansion of the Internet within the U.S. will certainly have a huge impact on the size and tenor of the Internet. As many other countries improve their internal networks and the connections between those networks and the Internet, more international expansion will occur.

Part of the Internet's magic is its unpredictability. A hundred years ago, the telephone was thought of as strictly a business tool; no one thought that every home would eventually have a phone in it. We have only had about a decade to think about what kind of information might be carried on the Internet, and even less time to consider how pervasive the Internet might become. With proposals like the NREN and the NII in the U.S., and similar proposals in other countries, the size and shape of the Internet will continue to change for many years.

STRUCTURE OF THE INTERNET

Creating a network of networks was a radical idea at the start. However, the Internet was so successful that the concept of internetworking, instead of having a single monolithic network, has become standard throughout the computer industry. It is useful to know a little about the structure of the Internet and how the individual user relates to it in order to see why it is amenable to rapid growth.

ARE YOU ON THE INTERNET?

Any computer that uses the TCP/IP networking protocol and is physically connected to another computer on the Internet is itself on the Internet. If the computer is on an "island" (either unconnected to any computer, or only connected to computers that are not connected outside the local network), it is not on the Internet.

CONNECTING TO THE BACKBONE

For many years, the NSFnet was called the *backbone* of the Internet. The backbone was a series of cable and connecting hardware that passed data at very high speeds. Figure 1.1 shows the structure of the old NFSnet backbone.

Recently, the NSF stopped running the backbone, and so many networks now have high-speed connections that connect to the remnants of the NFSnet that it is impossible to specify what is the Internet backbone and what isn't. However, the concept of the backbone

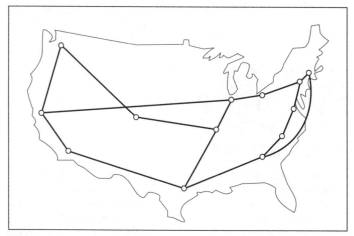

Figure 1.1: The old NSFnet backbone

still exists. Basically, the backbone is the central set of high-speed links, regardless of who owns the links. This set of links is growing rapidly, and it's harder and harder to determine what is "central" on the backbone.

Other computers connect directly to the backbone sites, and they usually also transmit data at high speeds. Other computers then connect to those, and so on, as shown in Figure 1.2.

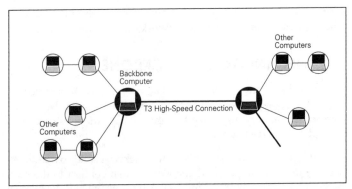

Figure 1.2: Making connections to the Internet backbone

Anything connected to the backbone, directly or indirectly, can be considered part of the Internet. As long as a single computer in one country is connected to another computer that is connected to the backbone, that country has access. It is only a matter of time before other computers in that country can connect through the first, or through additional connections. The more connections there are, the more likely it is that all users in that country can access the Internet more often. This is how the Internet has reached over 100 countries.

USERS: THE END OF THE TREE

It is useful to think of the backbone of the Internet as a forest. Each backbone site is a tree trunk. Off of that tree trunk come branches, each of which represents a computer attached directly to the backbone site. Off of those branches are sub-branches, representing computers that are connected to the computers that are connected to the backbone site. You can have many levels of sub-branches, and it doesn't matter how close a sub-branch is to the trunk of a particular tree: they are all part of the same forest. You can think of the Internet as the land that holds the trees up and defines the location of the forest.

So where do you, the Internet user, fit in? You are a leaf on the end of a sub-branch. Your sub-branch is the computer on which you have an account, as shown in Figure 1.3. Many computers have hundreds or thousands of user accounts on them, just as sub-branches have many leaves on them.

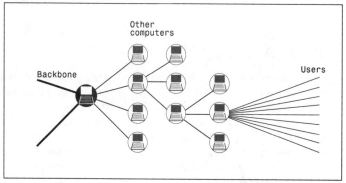

Figure 1.3: User connections to the Internet

PERSISTENT VS. INTERMITTENT CONNECTIONS

Most computers that are on the Internet are connected to the network all the time; these computers have a *persistent* connection. However, many computers have only an *intermittent* link to the Internet. If you have an intermittent link, your computer calls up another computer on the Internet, uses its connection for a while, then disconnects. This works well for users who only need to send mail back and forth through the Internet and do not care about how long it takes.

Intermittent connections are much less expensive to maintain than persistent connections. If the user only needs to transfer mail once a day, the computer can do it when the phone rates are the cheapest.

Even if the computer transfers mail every hour, it can save hundreds of dollars a month by not having a persistent telephone connection. Many computer bulletin board systems (also called *BBSs*) use various methods of intermittent connections to keep their costs down.

Persistent connection have advantages as well, and that is why most universities and many corporations have them. If your computer is located in a large city and there is another computer with a persistent connection in that city that allows such connections, staying on the Internet all the time can be fairly cost-effective, depending on how the telephone company charges for full-time leased lines. If you want to use the Internet for more than just mail, you want the computer that has your account to have a persistent connection.

SERVERS AND CLIENTS

Another important concept in understanding the structure of the Internet is that of *servers* and *clients*. A server is a computer that performs actions for another computer; a client is the computer that asks for the action. This is a broad definition, but an appropriate one: the range of the actions performed between a client and server is almost unlimited. The most important thing to keep in mind about the client/server relationship is that the client does not care *how* the server does the task, just that result is something the client wants.

For example, a client might ask a server to get a particular file. If the file is on the server computer, the server simply gets it from its disk and passes it back to the client. However, if the file is not on the server, but the server knows how to find it, the server finds the file and hands it back to the client. In both of these cases, the client got what is wanted: the file. If the server can't do what the client asks, the server must know the proper way to say that it can't, and hopefully will provide some information as to why.

This example is one of the simplest client/server interactions. A more complex action might be for the server to search a database and create a report on the results. Again, the client doesn't care what program the server uses to search the database or to make the report, and might not even care where the database resides. Assume that a user on computer C, the client, asks computer S, its server, for the results of a database search. Computer S may not know how to do the search, but it knows how to ask computer X how to do database searches. Computer X does the search using program A, creates a report using program B, and sends the report to S, which in turn sends the report to C. Note that S is the server to C, but S is also the client to X. This type of interaction is common on the Internet.

Such interactions may seem convoluted, but they make getting information from the Internet much easier. If you want an answer to a certain question, you don't really care whether the answer is on your computer or on a remote computer, and you really don't want to learn how to search for it. The more powerful and intelligent the server you connect to (or the more powerful and intelligent the server that your server becomes a client to), the more likely it is that you will get your answer quickly. By having thousands of intelligent systems on the Internet, finding answers becomes that much easier.

NAMING CONVENTIONS

With tens of thousands of computers and tens of millions of users, you would think that it would be almost impossible to differentiate between everyone. However, it is actually quite simple. Think about the U.S. postal system: you can get a message to any one of over 250 million people simply by knowing the fifteen or so words of a mailing address. The situation is almost identical on the Internet. When you get an account on a computer on the Internet, you get a two-part mailing address. The two parts are your account name and the address of the computer. The account name comes first, and the two are separated by an @ symbol.

For example, if you had a friend whose account name is `chrisr` and whose computer's address is `english.small.edu`, her mailing address would be `chrisr@english.small.edu`. Anyone on the Internet could send her mail at that mailing address without knowing where her computer is physically located, what kind of computer it was, or even whether or not her computer had a persistent or intermittent connection to the Internet.

 **See Also** *Addresses, Mail* in Part 2.

GETTING MESSAGES THROUGH

Given that all account names are unique, and all names on each level of the domain tree are unique, you can be sure that the combination of the two is also unique. The beauty of the scheme is that it makes passing messages between users incredibly simple. Your computer doesn't have to know how to reach every other computer on the Internet; it simply has to know how to be a good client to a computer that does know how to reach the desired recipient.

 See Also   *Domain Name System* in Part 2.

SECURITY

One of the things that makes the structure of the Internet so easy to expand is that there is virtually no inherent security in the Internet itself. Each computer is responsible for its own security, and there is no real inter-computer security on the Internet. This makes it is very easy for someone on the Internet to spy on transmissions undetected.

Instead of providing network-wide security, the Internet requires you, the user, to take responsibility for your own security. This is not difficult to do, but you would be surprised how many people don't take steps to maintain security and privacy.

There are two ways that security can be breached on the computer you use to connect to the Internet: by someone getting privileged access to all accounts on the computer, or by someone getting access to just one account. The former situation can be prevented by diligence on the part of the people who run the computer, using standard measures such as monitoring unsuccessful log-ins, but the latter can only be prevented by you. You should have a password that is hard to guess, you should change it often, and you should never tell your password to anyone.

 See Also   *Security* in Part 2.

WHO RUNS THE INTERNET?

Because it is so decentralized, no one "owns" or "runs" the Internet. Every computer that is connected to the Internet is responsible for its own part of the Internet, but not for any other part. In fact, no single company is responsible for maintaining the backbone. This means that if something doesn't work, you don't complain to "the management of the Internet." Instead, you talk to the system administrators for the computer you are on. If there is a connection problem, they will talk to the computer to which they are connected.

Having no one in charge is disconcerting for many people, and particularly for many companies who are used to always having someone to make things right when something doesn't work. On the other hand, if someone had been responsible at all times as the Internet grew, it is likely that the growth of the Internet would have been severely limited, and you wouldn't be reading this today.

The above description should not be interpreted to mean that the Internet is a free-for-all with no one guiding it. There are a few organizations who give the Internet some structure while creating a minimum number of restrictions. The unique environment in which the Internet sprang up makes these organizations different from the people who normally manage commercial networks.

INTERNET TECHNICAL GROUPS

Many volunteers helped bring a bit of order to the haphazard growth of the Internet. By the late 1980s, three major groups had formed to help coordinate and guide the technical parts of Internet, which was still almost completely supported by the NSF:

Abbreviation	Name
IETF	Internet Engineering Task Force
IRTF	Internet Research Task Force
IAB	Internet Architecture Board

The IETF develops and maintains the Internet's communication protocols, which are the methods by which computers on the Internet connect. The IRTF looks into long-term research problems, many of which will be critical to the Internet in five or ten years. The IAB oversees the IETF and IRTF and ratifies any major changes to the Internet that come from the IETF.

 **See Also** *Internet Architecture Board, Internet Engineering Task Force,* and *Internet Research Task Force* in Part 2.

INTERNET SOCIETY

The three groups discussed above mostly facilitate the technical structure and details of the Internet. As the Internet grew, many people became much more interested in what was happening on the Internet than in how the Internet was connected. In 1992, the Internet Society was formed to help connect the user-oriented people with the technical people.

See Also *Internet Society* in Part 2.

THE INTERNET AS A FRONTIER

The Internet is a sort of frontier—slightly lawless and with plenty of unclaimed space left to explore. Because of its lack of structure, the rules on the Internet are very different than the rules on commercial networks such as CompuServe. There is already an incredible amount of free information available on the Internet, and there will probably be hundreds of times more available within the next few years. The future will also bring a significant amount of information on the Internet for which you have to pay. There are local monitors on parts of the Internet, but if you don't like the local rules, you can move from one Internet access provider to another in a matter of seconds.

One group that is exploring the boundaries of the Internet and other computer-related areas is the *Electronic Frontier Foundation,* better known as the EFF. They study and support more realistic laws concerning the wilds of the electronic universe.

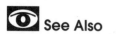 **See Also**   *Electronic Frontier Foundation* in Part 2.

MAJOR WAYS TO GET INFORMATION

Because the information on the Internet takes many forms, users look for different types of information in many ways. For example, you may have a simple question that you know has a one-sentence answer. Do you look for the answer in a file, do you ask someone who probably knows the answer, or do you pose the question to many people at once? Part of the choice depends on the type of question it is, part depends on whether you want to let others know you are asking the question, and another part depends on your personality.

Fortunately, the Internet supports many types of information gathering. If you are the kind of person who never wants to be public about your questions, you can anonymously search in many different areas for answers. On the other hand, if you like to make personal contact with those who give you answers, it is easy to pose questions to people directly without intruding on their daily schedules.

There are five primary methods for gathering information on the Internet. Each has a very different feel to it, and the results are also different. As you start to explore all five, you will probably find that you want to use different methods for different types of searching. Ahead is a very brief description of each method; they are all covered in much more depth in Part 2.

LISTINGS IN THE BOOK

To access different kinds of information, you must use different kinds of commands. Part 2 of this book covers the different commands and their uses. For each command, you must specify the location of the information in which you are interested.

When specific services or features on the Internet are listed in Part 2, they are followed by a brief description of how to access that service or feature. For instance, a reference in Part 2 might tell you that there is a Usenet news group that covers a particular subject; you need to know how to use Usenet news in order to get information from that source. (Usenet is described in Part 2.)

The following are examples for the types of references in this book. If you do not understand any of them, be sure to read the sections on the programs: Mail, Mailing Lists, Usenet News, ftp, Gopher, and WAIS. They are not described here because they are such large topics.

Many times, the same information will appear in many places on the Internet and will be accessible by different programs. In such a case, the reference in this book will probably be to a Gopher server in a well-known location (Gopher is also described in Part 2). Note that, if you cannot run a Gopher client program but can run **ftp**, most sites with Gopher servers also accept requests for anonymous ftp.

Mail

The most straight-forward method to get information is to ask a question to an individual you know has the answer. Assuming that the person obliges, your question gets a direct answer from someone you trust. The easiest way to ask this sort of question is to send it through mail. Then when that person gets your personal mail, he or she can decide when to respond, and how in-depth to make the answer.

Another advantage of personal mail is that it is easy to respond to, even if the recipient doesn't know you. Every mail program has a "reply" function that automatically opens and addresses a response letter to the person who mailed the original letter. Even if your Internet address is long and complicated, replying is usually painless, and sending a letter often costs nothing.

 **FOR MORE INFORMATION**

For example, you can send a letter to the President of the United States without a postage stamp:

Service:	**Mail**
Address:	`president@whitehouse.gov`
Subject:	*Whatever subject you wish*

Message: *Whatever you would normally say in a letter to the President*

Description: Letters to this address will be responded to just like letters sent on paper. Currently, responses come on paper, but that will probably change in the future. If you want to send a letter to the Vice President, the address is `vice.president@whitehouse.gov`.

Mailing Lists

Keeping abreast of a particular topic can be difficult if you rely on paper-based magazines and newsletters. A mailing list (also called a *mail group*) is a list of people who are interested in a particular topic and want to receive mail about it. The topics for some mailing lists are broad, such as privacy, while others are very narrow, such as motorcycle chassis design.

Mailing lists can be either *moderated* or *unmoderated*. Moderated lists have a leader who looks through each message, only passing along the ones that are relevant to the list; this cuts down the amount of mail that each member gets. Members of unmoderated lists, which are much more common, get everything that is sent to the list, regardless of its content. If you subscribe to too many mailing lists, you may get inundated with more mail than you can handle.

FOR MORE INFORMATION

For example, you may want to join a mailing list that discusses computer games:

Service: **Mailing List**

Name: The games list

Address: `listserv@brownvm.brown.edu`

Subject: *Any subject*

Message: subscribe games-l *your-name*

Description: This is a general discussion of computer
                  games.

Usenet News

One of the best way to keep informed on a particular subject is to
read the Usenet news group for that subject. The way Internet users
interact with Usenet news allows for better give-and-take conversations than mailing lists, but it is still somewhat unwieldy if the
topic is particularly active. Each person who says something has
his or her comments posted to the entire news group. You can
choose to reply to a message, and your reply message is associated
with the original. If another reader was not interested in the original comment, it is easy for them to skip over your reply.

Usenet news groups are one of the mainstays of the Internet. Like
mailing lists, they range from the serious to the silly. There are thousands of different topics. A few of them are moderated, but most are a
free-for-all (particularly the non-technical topics). Many topics are related to local geographic areas, so you can post an ad to sell your used
car and know that only people in your area will see your ad.

 **FOR MORE INFORMATION**

For example, you may want to read about hardware for PCs and
compatibles:

Service: **Usenet News**

Group: `comp.sys.ibm.pc.hardware.misc`

Description: Questions and answers on all hardware
                issues such as incompatibilities, new
                hardware, good prices, and so on.

Anonymous ftp

There are gigabytes worth of information stored in files that are
available to one and all on the Internet. To get to them, you use the
ftp program to connect to the computer on which they reside,
browse around, and then copy the files from the remote computer

to your own. This is one of the most direct ways of getting large amounts of public information. It is called anonymous **ftp** because you do not need to identify yourself in order to get access to the files.

Unfortunately, the **ftp** program is pretty unfriendly. Its user interface is extremely unhelpful, and its commands are cryptic. However, it may be the only method available to you for accessing particular files, so learning to use it is useful. A newer program, **ncftp**, is friendlier, but still difficult to use.

➡ FOR MORE INFORMATION

For example, you might want to get a guide to computer system security:

Service:	**Anonymous ftp**
Host:	`ds.internic.net`
Location:	/fyi/fyi8.txt
Description:	A handbook for Internet users on how to deal with security issues. It is a good beginning, but by no means comprehensive.

Gopher and WWW Servers

Because of **ftp**'s limitations, many new technologies for searching and browsing files have been developed in the past five years. The two that most common today are Gopher and WWW; in the next five years, others may replace these. Both have the same end result as **ftp**, namely to get you files that have the information you want, but they are much easier for novices (and even advanced users) to handle.

Both programs use the client/server model you learned about earlier. The machine on which the data resides must be running a server program for one of the programs. For example, to get access to files using a Gopher program, the computer with the files must be running the Gopher server software, and you must run the Gopher client program as well. Not all computers run all three servers, and in fact many don't run any of them yet. However, they will become more common as the servers become more popular.

FOR MORE INFORMATION

For example, you may want to get health information about cancer from the National Institutes of Health:

Service:	**Gopher**
Host:	`gopher.nih.gov`
Path:	Health and Clinical Information/CancerNet Information
Description:	This site has an extensive set of documents for physicians and patients on the dozens of types of cancer known to Western medicine. It also describes much of the ongoing cancer research, clinical trials, drug interactions, and so on.

FOR MORE INFORMATION

Or, you might want to find out about the U.S. Geological Survey:

Service:	**WWW**
URL:	`http://info.er.usgs.gov`
Description:	An overview of the USGS and geological research in general. The server has lots of information about geology at U.S. universities, and a small amount about corporate research. There are also still pictures and sound presentations.

YOUR CONNECTION TO THE INTERNET

There are many ways to get on the Internet. If you are on a network that is directly connected to the Internet, your interactions may be very different than if you use a modem to dial into such a computer. Once connected, your interactions may also be different.

CONNECTING DIRECTLY

Many people who work at universities are connected directly (with persistent connections) to the Internet through their campus-wide network. In fact, this was one of the goals of the early Internet: to let university scientists and researchers exchange information with other people across the country. Some companies also have persistent connections to the Internet. Due to security concerns, however, very few companies do this. Instead of connecting their in-house networks to the Internet, most companies require employees to make their Internet connections through a computer not on the company network.

USING A MODEM

Currently, the most common way to connect to the Internet is through a modem. You dial from a personal computer in your office or home to a host computer that is connected to the Internet. Most people only use their personal computers as intelligent terminals to connect to the host computer. In this case, your personal computer is not really on the Internet; instead, you are simply a user on the host computer.

It is also possible to have your personal computer networked to the host computer though the modem. When you network to the host (instead of just being a terminal), your computer appears to be on the Internet, and transferring files from the host computer and from other computers on the Internet is easier. There are two common protocols for doing this, called *SLIP* and *PPP*. (You don't need to know about the internals of these protocols, just that they allow you to connect as a TCP/IP computer over a serial line.) This method of connection is currently used by only a small number of people on the Internet, but will probably become much more common over the next few years.

Recently, some large commercial networks such as America Online and CompuServe have been offering Internet access as part of their services. If you have an account with one of these services, you have access to much more than just Internet mail. For example, both America Online and CompuServe give you full access to the World Wide Web, Usenet news, FTP, and so on. Thus, you may not need to get a separate account on an Internet-specific system if you are already using a commercial network. As the Internet becomes more popular, it is likely that other large networks will also give more than just mail access.

FINDING A CONNECTION SERVICE

If you are not yet on the Internet, your next question might be, "How do I find way to connect through my modem?" People who are affiliated with a university or company that has a direct Internet connection should check with their system administrator or support department on how to get a *dial-in* account (one that lets you connect to the network using a modem) on a computer that is on the Internet.

Most people, however, will have to find an Internet service provider or other kind of service that gives them the kind of access they want to the Internet. Fortunately, it is easy to find such providers. Even in smaller cities, there are often many choices for Internet connections, and millions of people have chosen nation-wide companies for their service. It's a good idea to shop around, rates can vary quite a lot from service to service.

Because you are dialing over the phone with your modem, it is important to find a service provider with a local phone number to reduce your telephone costs. There is speculation that in the near future competing local phone services will offer SLIP/PPP access for free.

Note that it is not necessary to be on the Internet if you only want to use personal mail. Many other commercial networks and bulletin board systems pass mail back and forth with people on the Internet. For example, if you have a CompuServe account, you can send and receive Internet mail.

CHARACTER-ORIENTED AND GRAPHICAL INTERFACES

Once you have connected to a computer on the Internet, you use various commands in order to interact with the computer. As you have probably noticed using your computer, program interfaces vary widely. Some are elegant and instantly understandable; others are functional but not terribly obvious; others are downright unfriendly and cryptic. The programs you can use to access information on the Internet fall into all three categories.

Many Internet users use programs with *character-based* interfaces, which means that you only see characters on your screen (no graphics, buttons, scroll bars, and so on). These programs work with any connection to the Internet, and are therefore the most widely used. A few of the popular programs, such as the Unix **mail** program and **ftp**, are *line-oriented* programs, meaning the commands and the results of the commands scroll up your screen a line at a time. More modern programs, such as some of the alternative mail programs and the Gopher client, are *screen-oriented*, meaning they assume that you have an 80 by 24 character screen and commands and results are put in different parts of the screen. Most people find screen-oriented programs easier to use than line-oriented programs.

More and more users interact with the Internet using graphical interfaces. If you have a SLIP or PPP connection from a PC or Macintosh to a host computer, or if you are directly connected to the Internet, you may have graphical programs that perform common tasks such as sending and receiving mail and reading Usenet news. There are many graphical programs that use the XWindows protocols that run on workstations. Although you can run XWindows over modems through SLIP and PPP, it is unlikely you would want to because of slow speeds.

This book covers both the graphical programs and character-based programs. However, there are more instructions for the character-based programs because they are often much more difficult to use than graphical programs. The two types of programs often have the same features with different interfaces, so the information in each will be of interest to many users.

LEARNING UNIX

Many of the computers that are on the Internet use the Unix operating system. In fact, almost all of the original Internet hosts were Unix-based. This forces many people to learn something about the Unix operating system in order to use the Internet. Unix is probably the least-friendly operating system still in wide use, which further complicates matters.

Today, fewer people have to interact with Unix, although the number is still significant. If you have a SLIP or PPP connection to the Internet, or connect through a service like CompuServe, consider yourself fortunate: you don't need to learn Unix. Even if you connect to a host computer and that computer does use Unix, there may be other methods for performing simple file manipulation, such as using a full-screen character interface or a graphical interface such as XWindows. If you are using line-oriented Unix interface, it is likely that the interface is either the *C shell* or the *Bourne shell*. (These are described in Part 2 under *Shells*.) Although many people are perfectly comfortable with these interfaces, they are often difficult for beginners (and even many intermediate-level users) to learn. If you are on Unix, ask your system administrator if there is a friendlier shell program that you can or should be using.

 See Also *Unix in Part 2.*

Part Two

Using the Internet

ABBREVIATIONS

Like many computer-based media, the Internet has its own language and jargon that pop up from time to time. It is likely that you will see many short-hand abbreviations in mail and in Usenet news postings.

This list describes some of the most common abbreviations. Many of them are meant to be sarcastic or at least humorous. For example, "I'll get to that RSN" usually means that it is a low priority.

Abbreviation	Meaning	Example
BTW	By the way	BTW, what time will you be there?
FAQ	Frequently-asked question; a list of common questions (and usually answers) for a topic	The PC communications FAQ covers this topic well.
FWIW	For what it's worth	We don't do that at my company, FWIW.
FYI	For your information	FYI, that model has been superseded by a less expensive one.
IANAL	I am not a lawyer; IANAD usually stands for "I am not a doctor"	IANAL, but I can't imagine that is legal.
IMHO	In my humble opinion	IMHO, it is a clearly superior program.

Abbreviation	Meaning	Example
OTOH	On the other hand	OTOH, I could be completely wrong…
ROTFL	Rolling on the floor, laughing	Excellent! ROTFL
RSN	Real soon now	They promised that they would ship it RSN.
RTFM	Read the fascinating manual! (This is usually stated in anger over a question that is answered in the documentation; you can substitute a common profane verbal adjective for the third word)	You can RTFM on that one.
YMMV	Your mileage may vary	It ran much faster on my computer; YMMV

 **FOR MORE INFORMATION**

Source:	**Anonymous ftp**
Host:	`ds.internic.net`
Path:	/fyi/fyi18.txt
Description:	Internet Users' Glossary, a list of abbreviations, acronyms, group names, jargon, and so on, all relating to the Internet.

See Also *Smileys*

ACCEPTABLE USE POLICY

Some networks on the Internet have policies that state what can and cannot be transmitted over those networks. The best known acceptable use policy (also called an *AUP*) was that of the NSFnet, which made up much of the Internet's U.S. backbone. Basically, the NSFnet policy was that you could use the network for information, research, and education, but not for for-profit business or extensive personal use. Other networks on the Internet do not have such restrictions.

Now that the NSFnet is no longer, there are very few "public" acceptable use policies. However, because of the increase of various types of commercial content on the Internet, there has been an increase in local policies. For example, your company might have a network-wide policy prohibiting the use of the company's Internet connection for playing games. Some companies and universities also prohibit certain kinds of speech over their networks.

ACROBAT

One of the problems that has always vexed the Internet is how to store the equivalent of printed pages from the Web on disk with the graphic images intact. It's not that this is hard to do: the problem has been that there are too many competing ways to do it. One method that has become popular (but by no means universal) is the Acrobat format, supported by Adobe Systems.

Adobe distributes free Acrobat viewing software that works with World Wide Web browsers. In fact, you can use this software even without using the Web. Many smaller companies hope that their page-display formats become as popular as Acrobat, but Adobe currently has the clear lead in market share.

ADDRESSES, COMPUTER

Every computer on the Internet has an address that can be viewed in two ways. The first one, the *domain name* (also called the *fully-qualified domain name*, or *FQDN*), is the computer's name in text, such as `mac.archive.umich.edu`. The domain name is used to send mail, make **ftp** requests, and so on. Before any message is sent out on the Internet, the domain name is converted to the second address, an *IP address*, which is a computer address that the computers on the Internet can deal with directly. Domain names are described in detail in Part 1.

Virtually all Internet commands take the domain name of a computer; only a few maintenance commands require the IP address. Thus, it is unlikely that you will ever need to know the IP address of any computer.

 **See Also**   *Domain Name System, IP Addresses*

ADDRESSES, MAIL

A mailing address for a user is made up of the user name, an @ symbol, and the domain name of the computer on which the user's account resides. For example, if someone's account name is `chrisr` and her computer's address is `english.small.edu`, her full mailing address would be `chrisr@english.small.edu`. If a person with whom you are communicating is on the same computer, you do not include the @ and the computer name: simply use the user's name by itself (such as `tomj` instead of `tomj@english.small.edu`).

How to Read a Mail Address

The first part of the address is easy: it's just the name you were assigned when you got an account on the system. Most names are short (eight characters or fewer), but some systems allow you to have long names. Names never have spaces in them and are usually all lowercase letters. No two accounts on a computer have the same name.

The computer address is a bit more complex. Every computer name on the Internet has at least one period in it, and many have two or three. The period, commonly pronounced "dot" when the name is spoken, separates the parts of the computer address. The left-most part of the computer address is the name of the computer; the right-most part of the address is called the top-level domain.

On the Internet, the top-level domain names are standardized so that mail can be routed easily. There are two types of domain names: *descriptive* and *locative*. Descriptive names tell the type of organization that the computer belongs to; the locative names tell the location of the computer. A computer address has one type of domain name or the other, never both.

These are the most common descriptive domain names:

Name	Description
com	Commercial businesses
edu	Educational institutions
gov	U.S. federal and state governments
mil	U.S. military
org	Miscellaneous organizations
net	Various types of networks

The locative names are always two-letter country abbreviations, such as *ca* for Canada and *jp* for Japan. Although they are not as common, you may also see domain names that end in *us* for locations in the United States.

Computer addresses are also like trees, with the top-level domain being the trunk (and the Internet as the whole forest). Each period denotes another sub-branch. At each level, there is an organization that chooses names for all the branches at the next level. In the example of the english.small.edu computer, the group that decides names for educational institutions (the "edu" people) named the computer "small", probably after the name of the university. At that university, there are probably several computers connected in a network; an administrator at the university decided the name of each computer, in this case "english".

Top-level domain names aren't always accurate. Many network access providers do not have "net" as their top-level domain name, a computer with a top-level domain name of "edu" may be used for commercial or military purposes.

How to Find a Mail Address

Finding a mailing address is usually quite difficult unless you know the name of the computer the person you are looking for is on. If you know that information, the program to try first is **finger**. The **finger** program tells you whether or not a person is on a particular computer. Use **finger** to look for a real name or a name that you think a person might use as an account name.

If **finger** yields no results, but you know the domain of a person's computer and a computer in that domain is running a *whois server*, you can use the **whois** program. At a university with many computers, for example, the whois server might have information for people on all the computers at that university. Only a small percentage of the computers on the Internet use whois servers, however. Many universities have other types of directory services, but it is difficult to know what service a site uses.

Another (fairly unreliable) method for finding an address is the M.I.T. Usenet user list. This is an *ad hoc* service through which you can find a person's mail address if she or he wrote messages to any Usenet group during a particular period of time. The computer at M.I.T. makes up a database of names and mailing addresses based on the information at the top of the news postings in many of the Usenet news groups. This is not a reliable way of finding a person because he or she may not have posted during the time covered in the database, or the person may not have used the name for which you are looking in the posting.

 **FOR MORE INFORMATION**

Source:	**Anonymous ftp**
Host:	`ftp.uu.net`
Location:	/usenet/news.answers/finding-addresses
Description:	An up-to-date reference on how to find mailing addresses on the Internet. This document lists many less-efficient searching mechanisms, such as Netfind and Knowbot, and has some good practical advice (such as trying to find the person by telephone and simply asking them).

◉ See Also   *finger*, *Netfind*, *whois*

ALT.

See Usenet News

AMERICA ONLINE

As a growing network that is still making a big impact, America Online (also known as *AOL*) is the largest commercial network that has extensive connections to the Internet. America Online allows its users to access most Internet services such as Usenet news groups and Gopher servers, and adds new Internet services often.

America Online is a large bulletin board system with its own interface software that runs on PCs and Macintosh computers. The interface is quite different than most bulletin board interfaces. Because of its graphical interface and pricing, America Online now has over one million users.

In late 1993, America Online introduced its Internet Center, an area that offers all America Online users direct access to the Internet. The introductory screen allows even a novice user quick access to all major Internet features. Figure 2.1 shows America Online's Web browser.

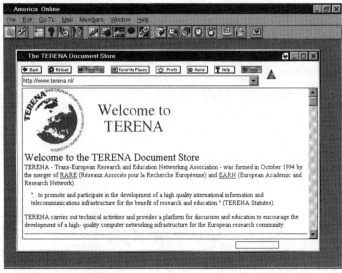

Figure 2.1: Using America Online to access the Web

 **See Also**   *Bulletin Board Systems*

AMIGA ARCHIVES

The Amiga computer is very popular for professional video production and high-quality arcade games. There are more users outside the U.S. than inside, and the sources of Amiga shareware and freeware reflect that.

How to Find Amiga Files

Many computers have a standardized set of Amiga files available for anonymous **ftp**. Within the U.S., these are the sites:

- `wcarchive.cdrom.com`
- `ftp.etsu.edu`
- `ftp.wustl.edu`
- `oes.orst.edu`

At each site, look for the /pub/aminet directory. Each site has the same files (they update each other automatically), so you only need to look in one place for any file.

ANONYMOUS FTP

See ftp, ncftp

ARCHIE

The best way to sort through the millions of files available by anonymous **ftp** is with **archie**, the gigantic database of all the files that are known to be publicly available. The **archie** database can't tell you the contents of the files, but if you know the name of the desired file and it is available, you can probably find it with **archie**. After you find the names and locations of the desired files, you use **ftp** or **ncftp** to get the files themselves.

The **archie** database system is maintained by many universities and networking organizations. Most run the same software, and all share information on the best ways of making the database available to the widest audience. Table 2.1 shows computers that have the archie database available. To reduce Internet traffic, choose the computer that is closest to you.

Table 2.1: Sites of **archie** servers

Computer	Location
`archie.ans.net`	ANS server, New York
`archie.internic.net`	AT&T server, New York
`archie.rutgers.edu`	Rutgers University, New Jersey
`archie.sura.net`	SURAnet server, Maryland
`archie.unl.edu`	U. of Nebraska
`archie.au`	Austrailia
`archie.univie.ac.at`	Austria
`archie.edvz.uni-linz.ac.at`	Austria
`archie.uqam.ca`	Canada
`archie.funet.fi`	Finland
`archie.th-darmstadt.de`	Germany
`archie.ac.il`	Israel
`archie.unipi.it`	Italy
`archie.kuis.kyoto-u.ac.jp`	Japan
`archie.wide.ad.jp`	Japan
`archie.kr`	Korea

Table 2.1: Sites of **archie** servers (continued)

`archie.sogang.ac.kr`	Korea
`archie.nz`	New Zealand
`archie.rediris.es`	Spain
`archie.luth.se`	Sweden
`archie.switch.ch`	Switzerland
`archie.ncu.edu.tw`	Taiwan
`archie.doc.ic.ac.uk`	United Kingdom

There are three ways to access the **archie** database:

- On your host computer with an **archie** client program
- Through mail
- By connecting to a computer with an **archie** server

How to Access archie on Your Host Computer

Of these three, the best method is to use an **archie** client program on your own computer, which is usually just called **archie**. The **archie** client lets you formulate a search, then sends that search over the Internet. This is more interactive than using mail and takes fewer of the Internet's resources (and the resources of the **archie** database computers) than connecting directly.

The results of all three methods are the same: a listing of all the sites that have files matching your request.

How to Use the archie Client

The **archie** client is a Unix command in which you give all the arguments on the command line; it then returns the matching list of files. The basic form of the command is a single argument (the file name you want to look for) such as

```
% archie manufacturing
```

This looks in the closest **archie** database for all files with the word *manufacturing* in the title and returns a list.

If the only argument you give is the search string, **archie** only lists files whose name is that exact string. To widen the search to files that have the string anywhere in their name, include the **-c** option, as in

```
% archie -c manufacturing
```

You might use this option when you know the subject you are looking for but not the specific name. If you are familiar with Unix regular expressions (which is a way of generalizing searches), you can use the **-r** option instead of **-c** to have **archie** treat the search string as a regular expression.

All options to the **archie** command are given before the search string. The main options are as follows:

Option	Description
-c	Looks for files with the specified string anywhere in their name.
-s	Same as -c, but ignores the case of letters in the search string.
-r	Treats the string as a regular expression. (You can only use one of the -c, -s, or -r options per search.)
-l	Changes the output to a list that can be read more easily by other computer programs. Each file in the list is on a single line that includes the date, size, site, and name of the file.
-t	Sorts the results so that the sites with the most recently-changed file is shown first. This is useful if you want find where the newest version of a file resides.

Option	Description
-L	Shows the names of the **archie** sites that were available when the copy of the **archie** program was compiled. It also tells which site is used as the default for searching.
-h *hostname*	Specifies which archie database host to use.
-m #	Sets the maximum number of files to list. The default, 95, may be more or less than you want to see. For example, to only see the first ten files found in the database, you would use the **-m 10** argument.
-N #	Sets the priority of the query from 0 (highest priority) to 32765 (lowest priority); the default is 0. If you think that the host is busy and your request is not that important, you should use this argument with a large number (that is, a lower priority).

 NOTE

There are **archie** clients for many other systems, many of which have a friendlier interface than the **archie** program described here. They usually have the same features as the Unix **archie** program.

How to Use archie by Mail

If you do not have an **archie** client available at your host, you can still get information back from the archie databases easily by using the second method: sending mail. You can send mail to any of the archie servers listed in Table 2.1; the server will read the mail and respond in the same format as for the **archie** client. The mail server replies by sending you mail with the results.

Each line of the mail message you send is a command. The possible commands in the message are as follows:

Command	Description
prog *string*	Searches the database for that string. This string is treated as a Unix regular expression (this should not matter to you for most searches).
path *mailad-dress*	Sends the output to the specified address instead of in a return message to you.
site *name*	Only searches the database for the named computer instead of all available computers.
compress	Compresses the output with the **compress** program, followed by the **uuencode** program. Only use this if you expect the output to be very long.
list *string*	Returns a list of all the computers in the database that match the string. If you don't include the string, all sites are listed.
servers	Sends back a list of all the available archie servers.
whatis *subject*	Returns an associated entry from the whatis database, a small database that has definitions used in some files.
help	Sends back information on using the mail server.
quit	An optional command to put at the end of your list.

FOR MORE INFORMATION

Source:	**Mail**
Address:	*Any archie site named in Table 2.1*
Subject:	*The subject line is ignored*

Message:	*Commands as described above*
Description:	The mail server will send you back a message with the results of the search.

How to Make a Direct Connection to an archie Server

Most **archie** servers also allow you to connect to them through the **telnet** program, the third method for accessing **archie**. Once you've logged into the server, you give commands to specify what you are interested in. This method is the slowest, wastes Internet resources, and prevents others from getting their requests filled by tying up the server.

Use the **telnet** program to connect to any of the archie servers listed in Table 2.1. When you are prompted to log in, key in the name **archie**. You are then prompted for commands.

The commands you give at the prompt are similar to the commands in the previous section on mailing to an archie server. The interactive commands are as follows:

Command	Description
set *variable value*	Sets the specified variable to the value. These are described below
show *variable*	Shows the value of the variable server
about	Gives a brief overview of archie
email	Tells how to use the mail interface to **archie**
quit	Exits the **telnet** program and returns you to your host computer. You can also use bye or exit to quit.

You probably don't need to use the **set** and **show** commands. If you do, use the **help set** command to get a list of the variables.

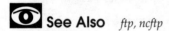 **See Also** *ftp, ncftp*

ARCHIVES

See Amiga Archives, Macintosh Archives, PC Archives, Unix Archives

ARPANET

The ARPAnet was the predecessor to the Internet. It gave networking researchers a practical opportunity to test the way long-distance networks respond in different environments. The ARPAnet was superseded by the NFSnet. The history of this change is described in Part 1.

ASCII

Computers internally deal with letters as numbers. The ASCII standard is by far the most popular way to translate from letters to the numbers computers use internally. ASCII stands for *American Standard Code for Information Exchange*.

Each 8-bit byte of computer memory has one of 256 values. The original ASCII table only specified the translation for the first 128 of those values; the other 128 were undefined. The characters in the original ASCII table are often called *ASCII values*.

All modern computers generate characters for all 256 values, which means that they generate more than just the ASCII values. Understanding this is important because some programs, such as many Unix mail programs, can only use ASCII values, not all 256 values. In many cases, you must be careful to only use ASCII values.

AUP

See Acceptable Use Policy

BANDWIDTH

Clearly, the speed of a network is important to all of its users. Network speed is measured as bandwidth, the amount of information that can be put in the network over a short period of time. The higher the bandwidth, the faster the network.

There are many common bandwidth speeds that you might have heard of. The bandwidth you can achieve depends on the kind of physical connection you have to the Internet.

14.4Kbaud	The speed of some modems sold today, but due to its slowness, on its way out.
28.2Kbaud	High-speed modems, necessary for sophisticated graphics on the Internet. Most new computers are shipping with this.
56Kbaud leased line	Common for businesses and Wide-Area Networks (WANs).
ISDN (Integrated Services Digital Network)	Now being offered by many phone companies, this can offer 56Kbaud or 128Kbaud, depending on the hardware.

T-1	Common for links between Internet servers; roughly 1500Kbaud, or 12 times faster than fast ISDN.
T-3	The speed of much of the Internet backbone; roughly 25 times faster than T-1.

BBS

See Bulletin Board Systems

BIND

The Berkeley Internet Name Domain (BIND) is an early implementation of the Domain Name System. Because it was distributed freely, BIND became the most common name server mechanism used on the Internet.

Because it is distributed freely and actively supported, BIND is the most common name server software on the Internet.

 See Also *Domain Name System*

BIT.

See Usenet News, BITNET

BITNET

Although tightly connected with the Internet, BITNET is an autonomous network of mostly academic and research sites. BITNET was being developed at the same time as the ARPAnet, but uses very different communications protocols. There are now many cross-links between the two nets, but there are still many major computers that are on BITNET and are not on the Internet.

Most of the computers on the BITNET are IBM and DEC mainframes. These computers do not allow remote login or file transfer. The BITNET network historically has been used mostly as a giant mail system. Because of this, the technology for mailing lists is more advanced on BITNET than it is on the Internet. The standard mailing list software, called *LISTSERV*, can handle large mailing lists with ease, and has many features for distributing files on request.

See Also   *Corporation for Research and Educational Networking, LISTSERV*

BOOKS, ON-LINE

The Internet is an excellent medium for storing and transmitting book-length material. The main restrictions are not technological, but legal. All books are automatically copyrighted as they are written, so the only ways you can freely distribute a book on-line are:

- if the copyright has expired, or

- if the copyright owner has given you permission

Fortunately, many books fall into both categories.

Two major projects are trying to get books freely available on-line: the Online Book Initiative and Project Gutenberg (both are described in their own separate sections in this book). Because there are no copyright restrictions on the books each distributes, there is some overlap between the two groups. The Online Book Initiative aims to get more current books that are freely distributable, while Project Gutenberg is making available more old classics whose copyrights have expired. There are on-line books all over the Internet, but these are two good places to start.

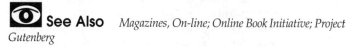 **See Also** *Magazines, On-line; Online Book Initiative; Project Gutenberg*

BOURNE SHELL

See Shell

BULLETIN BOARD SYSTEMS

Before access to the Internet became widely available, thousands of people set up computers in their homes to allow others to call in and exchange information. Today, there are over 10,000 of these bulletin board systems active in the U.S. alone, and the number continues to grow. Some are tiny, hosting maybe one or two dozen people, while others have tens of thousands of users and hundreds of incoming lines. Commercial systems like CompuServe and America Online can be thought of as very large bulletin board systems.

Bulletin board systems are important to the Internet because they are becoming increasingly connected to the Internet. It does not cost much for a bulletin board system operator (often called a *sysop*) to link the system to an Internet provider so that users can pass mail and read Usenet groups. Many larger systems have already done this, and dozens of smaller ones are doing so every month. Within a few years, most bulletin board systems will be part of the Internet.

One of the biggest attractions of bulletin board systems is that they offer services that are not on the Internet. For example, CompuServe has hundreds of file areas that are somewhat like anonymous **ftp** sites, but are much more structured. Services like the WELL have conversation areas that are also similar to some Usenet groups, but the regularity of the participants and the fact that responses are grouped and in time sequence makes the discussions easier to follow. Figure 2.2 shows one of the many files on America Online.

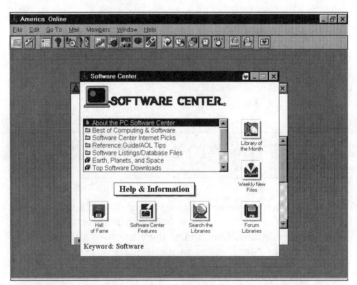

Figure 2.2: America Online's file areas

Small bulletin boards have a much different feel than the larger ones, and a very different feel from the Internet. When only 50 or 100 people can participate in a particular discussion, you get more of a sense of community than when millions can. Most bulletin boards are free, so connecting to them is easier for beginners who are not sure they want to commit to monthly fees.

An excellent resource on bulletin board systems is *Boardwatch* magazine. The print edition is available at many magazine shops, and they have an excellent Web server.

 **FOR MORE INFORMATION**

Service:	**WWW**
URL:	`http://www.boardwatch.com`
Description:	The latest issue of Boardwatch as well as other useful Internet information.

See Also   *America Online, AppleLink, CompuServe, Prodigy, the WELL*

C SHELL

See Shell

CAMPUS-WIDE INFORMATION SYSTEM

Universities and colleges were the first major non-defense users of the Internet. To reduce the support load for these systems, many campus administration centers set up campus-wide consultant offices. These offices often provided unified electronic bulletin boards for campus events, easily-searchable campus directories, message boards, and other features. Universities worked together to make these systems work, and many adopted the name *Campus-Wide Information System*, or *CWIS* for short. Higher education computer groups helped pool CWIS resources to reduce the amount of repetition among colleges.

CARL

In the late 1980s, universities began to see the Internet as an excellent distribution medium for academic information such as journal articles. The Colorado Alliance of Research Libraries, better known as *CARL*, started making the tables of contents of thousands of academic journals available for free. The easiest way to access CARL is through the Internet. CARL, through its for-profit UnCover program, allows its users to search through their table of contents and abstracts databases, find the articles that they are interested in, and get those articles faxed to them for a fee.

FOR MORE INFORMATION

Service:	**Mail**
Address:	`help@carl.org`
Subject:	*Any subject line*
Message:	*A request that includes your postal mail address or fax number*
Description:	CARL will send a brief overview of their services. They will also mail or send to you by fax more information (they do not have this information available on-line).

CATALOGS

See Library Catalogs

CERN

The World Wide Web was born in Switzerland in the early 1990s, at a physics research center commonly known as CERN. CERN, the European Laboratory for Particle Physics, was interested in setting up a research network that physicists from around the world could share to publish research information as it was developed. The initial work at CERN quickly moved beyond the physics world, and CERN handed over its Web development to other organizations. (CERN is an acronym for the center's old name in French, Conseil Europeen pour la Recherche Nucleaire.)

CERT

See Computer Emergency Response Team

CHAT

The **chat** program was popular on the Internet many years ago, but has been superseded by the more interesting **irc** (Internet Relay Chat) program. Basically, **chat** lets you talk on-line to many people at the same time. The **irc** program has a much better interface and has therefore replaced **chat** on most systems.

 **See Also** *Internet Relay Chat*

CIX

See Commercial Internet Exchange

CLARINET

ClariNet is the primary vendor of on-line, international news for the Internet community. For a fee, ClariNet makes many different kinds of news available through Usenet news at your site.

You must pay ClariNet Communications Corp. to get the ClariNet news on your computer system; it is not a free service. However, many services that provide Internet connections have licenses for the ClariNet news feed, so that their users have unrestricted access to that system. Some universities and freenets also get the ClariNet news feed.

The on-line newspaper published by ClariNet includes national and local news from the UPI news wire, often within a few hours of its appearance; additional news such as sports, business, science, and weather; news specific to the technology industries; stock prices; and some syndicated columns.

If your host system gets the ClariNet news, you can find the information in the Usenet news under the clari. heading.

 **FOR MORE INFORMATION**

Service:	**Mail**
Address:	info@clarinet.com
Subject:	*Any subject*
Message:	*Any request for information*
Description:	Use this mail address to get more information about getting a ClariNet news feed for your system.

See Also   *Usenet News*

CLEARINGHOUSE FOR NETWORKED INFORMATION DISCOVERY AND RETRIEVAL

In 1992, the National Science Foundation funded the Clearinghouse for Networked Information Discovery and Retrieval, better known as *CNIDR*, to study and coordinate the tools being used for searching and retrieving information off the Internet and other large networks. Its objectives include the following:

- to promote and support the implementation and use of networked information discovery and retrieval software applications such as WAIS, Gopher, and World Wide Web

- to coordinate and create consensus among developers of searching tools to ensure compatibility and interoperability

- to disseminate information about applications to the Internet community as well as to those active with networked information applications development

- to collect and create documentation and manuals, project information, binaries and source code, bibliographies, and general information on the search tools

- to classify protocol standards and compliance; identify, classify, and integrate noteworthy projects; and identify and cross-reference provider and consumer communities both on an off the Internet

CNIDR is making some tools more available. They are distributing freeWAIS, a non-commercial implementation of the WAIS server, and are helping develop other software in conjunction with different groups. CNDIR also gives seminars to groups trying to find their way through all of the different information technologies.

 **FOR MORE INFORMATION**

Service:	**WWW**
URL:	`http://cnidr.org/welcome.html`
Description:	This World Wide Web server has information on CNIDR's current projects, future plans, and so on.

CLIENT

A client is a program that asks a server program for an action. Clients and servers are described in Part 1.

CNIDR

See Clearinghouse for Networked Information Discovery and Retrieval

COMMERCENET

Businesses are flocking to the Internet, but many of them do not understand the technology of the Internet or how it will affect their business. CommerceNet is a broad-ranged industry consortium whose primary goals are to help businesses understand what on-line commerce is about and to do research into various areas of online commerce. CommerceNet's members range from small companies to the largest of banks, and it has members throughout the world.

FOR MORE INFORMATION

Service: **WWW**

URL: `http://www.commerce.net/`

Description: CommerceNet makes many documents
              about on-line commerce available to the
              general public at its Web site. The site
              also has links to CommerceNet's members'
              Web pages.

 **See Also**   *Online Commerce*

COMMERCIAL INTERNET EXCHANGE

Until a few years ago, no purely commercial traffic was allowed on the Internet because of the NSFnet's Acceptable Use Policy. That has changed, and there are many networking companies that support commercial use of the Internet. These service providers often do not allow users to log into them directly; instead, they sell Internet bandwidth to companies that allow logins.

The Commercial Internet Exchange (better known as *CIX*) was for a while the most powerful coordination group in the United States. However, the changeover to an all-commercial Internet caused CIX to lose much of its stature, although it still represents its members in lobbying and promotional activities.

 **FOR MORE INFORMATION**

Service:	**Mail**
Address:	info@cix.org
Subject:	*Any subject*
Message:	*Any request for information*
Description:	Use this mail address to get more information concerning CIX.

COMP.

See Usenet News

COMPRESS

Although people move files around on the Internet as if such movement is free, every file transfer uses some network resources. If you are moving large files using **ftp**, it is often better to compress files before you move them. Compressing a file (sometimes called compacting, stuffing, or shrinking) generally makes it half as large; for graphics files, compression can make the file $\frac{1}{20}$ of the original size. After you move the file, uncompress it with a companion program.

Compression programs find and eliminate redundant information in a file, marking where the redundancy occurred. A standard text file can usually be compressed by half, program files by a third, and other files by varying amounts. File compression only works on uncompressed files, such as text files and programs. If you try to compress a file that is already compressed, the resulting file may be larger than the original. Some types of files, such as images stored as GIF files, are already internally compressed.

There are dozens of programs for compressing files in different ways. The most common compression program on Unix systems is **compress**, and the matching uncompression is called **uncompress**. Another popular pair of compression programs is **gzip** and **gunzip**.

The **compress** program takes a single argument: the name of the file to be compressed. The result is a file with the same name but with .Z at the end. It removes the original (large) file and replaces it with the compressed file.

 NOTE

The original file is deleted and replaced with the compressed file. You should only use **compress** with files that you do not need to access in their uncompressed forms.

⇉▶ FOR MORE INFORMATION

Service:	**Anonymous ftp**
Host:	`ftp.cso.uiuc.edu`
Location:	/doc/pcnet/compression
Description:	An excellent list of all the compression schemes in common (and not-so-common) use on PCs, Macintosh systems, Unix, IBM mainframes, and Amiga computers. It also tells where to get the freeware and shareware programs.

COMPUSERVE

CompuServe has been a major commercial network for over fifteen years. It has one of the largest subscriber bases in the world and offers an incredible number of services, including on-line airline ticket ordering, customer support for dozens of major computer vendors, magazines, extensive shopping opportunities, and so on.

CompuServe has recently made a major plunge into the Internet services market by allowing its members full access using their own Web browser. This access is similar to local SLIP and PPP accounts, and gives CompuServe members a good taste for what's on the Internet. CompuServe has also bought many Internet-related companies in an effort to be a full-service provider. Figure 2.3 shows CompuServe's Internet service offerings.

Most CompuServe accounts are two numbers separated by a comma, such as **41325,3467**. To send mail to someone with this kind of CompuServe account, change the comma in their account number to a period and give **compuserve.com** as the machine name. Thus, this type of mailing address might be **41325.3467@compuserve.com**. Recently, CompuServe has allowed its members to also use alphabetic names like other Internet services.

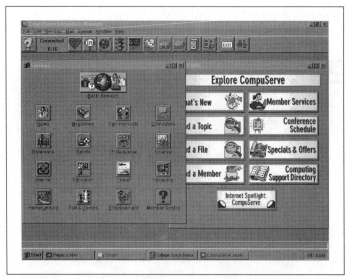

Figure 2.3: Accessing the Internet through CompuServe

COMPUTER EMERGENCY RESPONSE TEAM

Security is a major concern to many people on the Internet. The Computer Emergency Response Team (better known as *CERT*) was formed to deal with security issues. CERT is funded by the Defense Advanced Research Projects Agency (DARPA) to serve as a central information point for all known security vulnerabilities of computers on the Internet. They also have a 24-hour hotline for security incidents and prepare newsletters about security to alert system operators and users of the various problems they might face.

Each time a potential security breach is verified by CERT, they send out an advisory describing the problem and (hopefully) how to solve it. For example, if a particular version of one vendor's Unix operating system allows people to get access to files that they should not have, the advisory tells how such access could take place and offers steps to take to prevent the access. CERT also supports a mailing list that discusses software and hardware that can be used to increase security.

 **FOR MORE INFORMATION**

Service:	**Anonymous ftp**
Host:	`cert.org`
Location:	`/pub`
Description:	This directory contains many files concerning security in general. The info directory has many books and papers that you can read. The advisories directory has all of the advisories that have been issued to date. Other directories have programs that can detect security problems (and help prevent them), discussions of PC and Macintosh viruses, and so on.

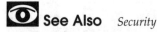 **See Also**   *Security*

CONSORTIUM FOR SCHOOL NETWORKING

The Internet has caught the eye of teachers and education administrators throughout the United States. The Consortium for School Networking, better known as *CoSN*, wants to get networking resources to teachers and students in K-12 schools.

CoSN, a non-profit organization, hopes to bring commercial educational vendors into the planning stages of the National Research and Education Network (NREN) so that the result isn't all commercial or all government-sponsored. CoSN also wants to be sure that the resulting network is for everyone in K-12 education, not just administrators.

FOR MORE INFORMATION

Service:	**WWW**
URL:	`http://www.cosn.org`
Description:	Contains files explaining how to join and help the organization, position papers on the current state of the Internet and K-12 education, state and local projects, and many other topics.

Service:	**Mail**
Address:	`membership@cosn.org`
Subject:	*Any subject*
Message:	*Any request for information*
Description:	Use this mail address to get more information about accessing CoSN and their services.

See Also *Education Resources, National Research and Education Network*

CORPORATION FOR RESEARCH AND EDUCATIONAL NETWORKING

The Corporation for Research and Educational Networking, better known as *CREN*, oversees the BITNET and its structure. Joining CREN and participating in the BITNET gives you access to many sites that are not directly on the Internet. Because many BITNET sites are colleges and universities, CREN also serves as a focal point for discussing networking among universities and colleges.

FOR MORE INFORMATION

Service:	**WWW**
URL:	`http://www.cren.net/`
Description:	Files listing all the BITNET members, a description of the benefits of joining CREN, and recent CREN newsletters.

Service:	**Mail**
Address:	`cren@bitnic.educom.edu`
Subject:	*Any subject*
Message:	*Any request for information*
Description:	Use this mail address to get more information about accessing CREN and their services.

 **See Also** *BITNET*

COSN

See Consortium for School Networking

CPIO

The **cpio** command makes whole directories into one file, keeping the directory structure intact. To unbatch a file that is stored with **cpio**, give the command with the **-icd** argument, followed by a < and the name of the file. For example, if the file you are unbatching is called design.cpio, use the following command:

```
% cpio -icd < design.cpio
```

CREN

See Corporation for Research and Educational Networking

CWIS

See Campus-Wide Information System

CYBERCASH

See Online Commerce

DDN

See Defense Data Network

DEFENSE DATA NETWORK

The U.S. military was the early developer and supporter of the Internet and still uses it extensively for communications. The military is aware of the security risks of using an inherently insecure medium, and they support research on making communications over the Internet more secure for all users.

The Defense Data Network, also known as the *DDN*, is the U.S. military's general computer network system. Parts of the DDN overlap with the Internet, while others are on separate networks with only limited exchange with the Internet. MILNET, which is a part of the DDN that was previously part of the Internet, is a separate network with controlled data exchange.

DIALOG

Although many databases can be accessed for free on the Internet, hundreds of commercial databases are not free. The largest supplier of commercial databases is DIALOG. As a DIALOG customer, you can access databases over the Internet using the **telnet** program to connect to dialog.com. DIALOG charges a small amount for Internet access, less than it charges for using other networking services.

 **FOR MORE INFORMATION**

Service: **WWW**

URL: `http://www.dialog.com`

Description: This server includes detailed instructions on accessing DIALOG databases, lists of all the databases arranged by subject, connection hints, and so on.

DIRECTORY SERVICES

See White pages, Yellow pages

DNS

See Domain Name System

DOMAIN NAME SYSTEM

The Domain Name System, better known as *DNS*, translates computer names into their associated IP addresses (the numerical address internally used for sending messages), so that you don't need to know the IP address of a computer.

If you do want to know the IP address, use the **nslookup** command (although this command is not available to users on all systems). Give the command with the command-line argument of the desired computer.

e.g. EXAMPLE

If you want to know the IP address of the computer called ivideo.com, use the following command:

```
% nslookup ivideo.com
Server:   uucp1.small.edu
Address:  196.201.90.0

Non-authoritative answer:
Name:     ivideo.com
Address:  204.1.1.23
```

👁 **See Also**   *Addresses, Computer; BIND; IP Addresses*

DOWNLOADING

See File Transfers

EARN

See TERENA

E-CASH

See Online Commerce

ECONET

The EcoNet is a bulletin board system linking many non-profit organizations and individuals concerned with environmental preservation. It was one of the first systems that brought together diverse local groups to discuss local problems in a national venue. The discussions on EcoNet span the entire range of environmental issues, from energy policy to grass-roots organizing.

If you want to send mail to someone on EcoNet, use the person's account name and the machine name **igc.apc.org**. Thus, you might send mail to `chrisr@igc.apc.org`.

 **FOR MORE INFORMATION**

Service:	**WWW**
URL:	http://www.econet.apc.org/econet/
Description:	A great deal of information about EcoNet, news items about ecology, and links to other ecology groups on the Internet, as well as links to other igc networks like Peacenet, LaborNet, WomensNet, and ConflictNet.

 **See Also**   *igc, PeaceNet*

EDUCATIONAL RESOURCES INFORMATION CENTER

The Educational Resources Information Center (better known as *ERIC*) is a network of computers that provides access to many education-related resources. One of its best resources is AskERIC, a project to develop and study Internet-based education information services, systems, and resources for K-12 end users. ERIC is a federally-funded program.

AskERIC's best benefit is that you don't have to do all the searching yourself: you can send mail to the staff and get an answer within a day or two. This, plus the Gopher server for those who like to look themselves, allows AskERIC to serve both those just starting on the Internet and those who are already familiar with it.

 **FOR MORE INFORMATION**

Service:	**WWW**
URL:	http://ericir.syr.edu/
Description:	Lots of answers to common questions from teachers and parents, as well as information on how you can ask specific questions not answered on the Web site.

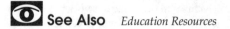 **See Also**   *Education Resources*

EDUCATION RESOURCES

Although colleges and universities get the lion's share of attention on the Internet, primary and secondary schools (commonly called *K-12* schools) have started making their presence known on the Internet. The Internet is a low-cost way for teachers to network and for students to learn research methods. Many organizations, such as the Consortium for School Networking and the Corporation for Research and Educational Networking, have emerged to help K-12 schools get on the network and use it effectively.

This section lists just a few of the hundreds of resources available for people interested in K-12 education. There is a complete guide to education resources that is being prepared as this book is being written. It should soon be available as an Internet FYI document.

Mailing Lists

Service:	**Mailing List**
Name:	CoSNdisc
Address:	`listproc@list.cren.net`
Subject:	*Blank*
Message:	subscribe cosndisc *your name*
Description:	Discussion of CoSN and its members.

Service:	**Mailing List**
Name:	K12admin
Address:	`listserv@suvm.syr.edu`
Subject:	*Blank*
Message:	subscribe k12admin *your name*
Description:	Discussion of the problems of K-12 administrators.

Web Servers

Service:	**WWW**
URL:	`http://web66.coled.umn.edu/`
Description:	Web66 is a marvelous collection of information on how K-12 classrooms can get on the Internet and what they can expect when they get there.

Service:	**WWW**
URL:	`http://gsn.org/gsn/gsn.home.html`
Description:	The Global SchoolNet Foundation (GSN) explains what kind of content K-12 kids can expect to find on the Internet and helps link classrooms from around the world to each other.

Usenet News Groups

All of the groups in the `k12.` hierarchy deal with education. However, some computers do not carry these Usenet groups. Other relevant news groups include those that begin with misc.education and misc.kids.

👁 **See Also** *Consortium for School Networking, Corporation for Research and Educational Networking, Educational Resources Information Center*

EDUCOM

Colleges and universities have long been leaders in adapting computer technology to the needs of students. EDUCOM, formed in 1964, helps higher educational institutions use computer technology in all areas, including the classroom, the research lab, and in administration. In the past ten years, EDUCOM has taken a leading role in getting universities the best access to networks such as the Internet. They were major proponents of the National Research and Education Network (NREN).

⇛ FOR MORE INFORMATION

Service:	**WWW**
URL:	`http://www.educom.edu`
Description:	This server has hundreds of files of interest to the higher education community. You can also find information about EDUCOM members and how your college can become a member.

Service:	**Mail**
Address:	`info@educom.edu`
Subject:	*Any subject*
Message:	*Any request for information*
Description:	Use this mail address to get more information about joining EDUCOM and accessing their services.

EE

One of the easiest-to-use editors for Unix is **ee**. It is not as popular as other full-screen editors, such as **emacs** or **joe**, but its popularity is increasing because of its simple interface. If you don't want advanced editing features, **ee** is a good choice.

ee is a *modeless* editor, meaning that anything you type is inserted in your document. All commands are given by pressing a Ctrl-*key*

sequence or by pressing Esc. If you have →, ←, ↑, and ↓ keys, you
can also use them. Figure 2.4 shows the way editing with **ee** looks
on-screen. The editing keys are fairly easy to learn. Table 2.2 lists
the Ctrl keys you use to edit.

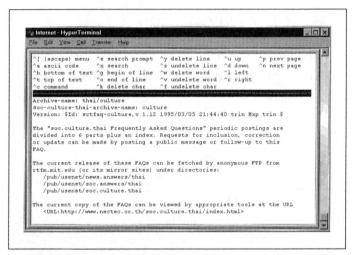

Figure 2.4: ee editing screen

Table 2.2: ee editing keys

Key	Action
Ctrl-a	Prompt for the ASCII value of a character to insert
Ctrl-b	Go to the bottom of the text
Ctrl-c	Get the prompt for an extended command
Ctrl-d	Go down one line
Ctrl-e	Prompt for a search string
Ctrl-f	Undelete the last deleted character
Ctrl-g	Go to the beginning of the line
Ctrl-h	Erase character to the left
Ctrl-i	Insert a Tab character
Ctrl-j	Insert a newline

Table 2.2: ee editing keys (continued)

Key	Action
Ctrl-k	Delete the character the cursor is on
Ctrl-l	Go left one character
Ctrl-m	Insert a newline character
Ctrl-n	Go to the next page
Ctrl-o	Go to the end of the line
Ctrl-p	Go to the previous page
Ctrl-r	Go right one character
Ctrl-t	Go to the top of the text
Ctrl-u	Go up one line
Ctrl-v	Undelete the last deleted word
Ctrl-w	Delete the word beginning at the cursor position
Ctrl-x	Search
Ctrl-y	Delete from the cursor position to the end of the line
Ctrl-z	Undelete the last deleted line
Ctrl-[	Show pop-up menu

Some of **ee**'s features are commands that require more than a single keystroke. These are accessed through the pop-up menu. Pressing Esc brings up the pop-up menu. Use the ↑ and ↓ keys to move in the pop-up menu, then press ↵ when you have selected the submenu you want. The choices are shown below.

Option	Description
leave editor	Quits **ee**, prompting you to save the file if you haven't already done so
help	Displays help information
file operations	Allows you to read, write, save, and print files
redraw screen	Redisplays the screen

Option	Description
settings	Specialized settings, described below
search	Finds particular characters in your file
miscellaneous	format, shell, check

The settings are as follows:

Option	Description
tabs to spaces	Converts each Tab character to five spaces
case-sensitive search	Allows you to make the searches for exact capitalization
margins observed	Allows you to cut off any text that appears beyond the right margin
auto-paragraph format	Specifies whether or not to automatically wrap paragraphs at the end of each line
eightbit characters	Tells whether to specify characters outside the ASCII codes as numbers or characters
info window	Tells whether or not to display the commands at the top of the screen
right margin	Specifies the right margin

EFF

See Electronic Frontier Foundation

ELECTRONIC FRONTIER FOUNDATION

As discussed in Part 1, the Internet (and indeed all of the networked world) is something of a frontier. There are only a few laws, and those are not well enforced. There is a lot of territory, and some people are already making life difficult for the early settlers. The Electronic Frontier Foundation (*EFF*) is a group that wants to be sure that the original intentions of the U.S. Constitution and the Bill of Rights are kept alive on the network, at least the part in the U.S. The EFF is a membership organization that lobbies in favor of basic freedom for everyone on the networks.

In their own words:

> "From the beginning, EFF has worked to shape our nation's communications infrastructure and the policies that govern it in order to maintain and enhance First Amendment, privacy and other democratic values. We believe that our overriding public goal must be the creation of Electronic Democracy, so our work focuses on the establishment of:
>
> - new laws that protect citizens' basic Constitutional rights as they use new communications technologies,
>
> - a policy of common carriage requirements for all network providers so that all speech, no matter how controversial, will be carried without discrimination,
>
> - a National Public Network where voice, data and video services are accessible to all citizens on an equitable and affordable basis, and
>
> - a diversity of communities that enable all citizens to have a voice in the information age."

In addition, the EFF sponsors litigants in legal cases in which they believe civil rights have been violated, supports the establishment of networks that carry all information regardless of content, supports giving free and wide access to U.S. public documents, is advocating ISDN service as a method to make interactive computing available to everyone, and is active in many other areas.

 **FOR MORE INFORMATION**

Service:	**WWW**
URL:	`http:\\www.eff.org`

Description: The server contains all documents that
                have been produced by the EFF and other
                affiliated groups.

Service: **Mail**

Address: `eff@eff.org`

Subject: *Any subject*

Message: *Any request for information*

Description: You can use this mailing address to get a
                membership form or to get on the mailing
                list for the EFF's newsletter.

ELECTRONIC MAIL

See Mail

ELM

elm has become one of the preferred mail programs on Unix systems because of its ease of use and power. It is a full-screen program that lets you organize your incoming and outgoing mail. For intermediate and advanced users, **elm** also offers a wide range of configuration features.

Figure 2.5 shows the main **elm** screen, also called the *index window*. Each line in the middle of the **elm** screen is a mail message to you.

The columns of information are as follows:

- The status of the mail

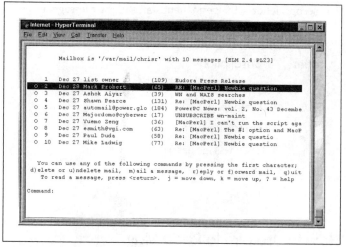

```
  Internet - HyperTerminal                                    _ □ ×
 File  Edit  View  Call  Transfer  Help


         Mailbox is '/var/mail/chrisr' with 10 messages [ELM 2.4 PL23]


      1   Dec 27  list owner        (109)  Eudora Press Release
   O  2   Dec 28  Mark Probert      (65)   RE: [MacPerl] Newbie question
   O  3   Dec 27  Ashok Aiyar       (39)   WN and WAIS searches
   O  4   Dec 27  Shawn Pearce      (131)  Re: [MacPerl] Newbie question
   O  5   Dec 27  automail@power.glo (184) PowerPC News: vol. 2, No. 43 Decembe
   O  6   Dec 27  Majordomo@cyberwer (17)  UNSUBSCRIBE wn-maint
   O  7   Dec 27  Yuemo Zeng        (36)   [MacPerl] I can't run the script aga
   O  8   Dec 27  esmith@vgi.com    (63)   Re: [MacPerl] The #! option and MacP
   O  9   Dec 27  Paul Duda         (58)   Re: [MacPerl] Newbie questio
   O  10  Dec 27  Mike Ladwig       (77)   Re: [MacPerl] Newbie question


    You can use any of the following commands by pressing the first character;
  d)elete or u)ndelete mail,  m)ail a message,  r)eply or f)orward mail,  q)uit
    To read a message, press <return>.  j = move down, k = move up, ? = help

 Command:
```

Figure 2.5: elm main screen

- The message number

- The date it was mailed

- Who mailed it

- The number of lines in the message

- The subject

If you have more than ten messages in your mailbox, only ten lines appear on the screen, but you can see additional pages of message lines, as described below.

There are two letters in the status section of the message lines. The first letter can be one of the following:

Letter	Description
D	Waiting to be deleted
E	Expired
N	New message
O	Old message (one that you have seen listed in **elm** but have not read)

The second letter is the permanent status of the message, meaning the status that came with it. The second letter can be one of the following options:

Letter	Description
A	An action is associated with the message
C	Confidential
F	Form letter
M	The message has MIME content
P	Private
U	Urgent

How to Use elm to Read Mail

The choices at the bottom of the screen are the commands that you can give to **elm**. (There are many commands that are not listed on the screen; they are described later in this section.) Use the first letter of the commands to activate them, such as **r** to reply to a message. To select which message to act on, use the ↑ and ↓ keys. If you have more than ten messages and you press the ↓ key on the bottom line, you will see the next set of ten messages.

For example, to read the third letter, press the ↓ key until the arrow is next to it and then press ↵. Instead of using the ↑ and ↓ keys, you can type the message number and press ↵. This is useful if you have many messages.

As you are reading a message, the screen shows a great deal of information other than just the content of the message. The top of the message, called the *header,* has all of the mailing information that came with the message, including who sent it, when it was sent, the subject, and so on. The header sometimes goes on for many lines.

The prompt at the bottom of the mail reading window has one of two forms.

- If the message is short and fits on a single screen, the prompt is *Command ('i' to return to index):*.

- If the message is longer than a single screen, the prompt says something like *There are 208 lines left (12%). Press <space> for more, or 'i' to return.*

In both these cases, you have commands to choose from. They are listed in Table 2.3, with the most common commands listed first.

Table 2.3: elm mail reading commands

Key	Meaning
Space	If you are paging through the message, this will display the next screen of the current message. If you are at the end of a message, it shows the first screen of the next message.
q	If you are paging through the message, quit pager mode and return to the index screen.
r	Reply to just the author of the message.
g	Reply to all recipients of the message. Note that this might send mail to many people.
d	Delete the message and display the next undeleted message. (You can undelete it in the main menu if you do this by mistake).
t	Tag the message for further operations. When you return to the index, all items that are tagged have a + in front of their message numbers.
s	Save the message or tagged messages to a folder.
f	Forward the message to another person. **elm** lets you edit the message you are forwarding if you wish.
m	Create a new mail message.
j, n, ↓	Advance to next undeleted message.
J	Advance to next message, regardless of status.
k, ↑	Go back to previous undeleted message.
K	Go back to previous message, regardless of status.
u	Undelete the message.
i	Return to index screen.

Table 2.3: elm mail reading commands (continued)

Key	Meaning
p	Print the message or tagged messages on host computer's printer.
!	Shell escape.
>	Save the message or tagged messages to a folder.
C	Copy the message or tagged messages to a folder.
b	Bounce the message (similar to forwarding).
h	Display headers with message.
|	Pipe the message or tagged messages to a system command.
<	Scan the message for calendar entries.
x	Exit with prompt, leaving folder untouched.
X	Exit without prompt, leaving folder untouched.
Return	If you are at the end of a message, it shows the message again. If you are in the pager, it shows just the next new line of the message. This is rarely used.

e.g. EXAMPLE

Assume that you have read a letter and you want to send it to someone else before deleting it. Press **f** to forward it, enter the name of the recipient, edit the forwarded message if you wish, then return to this screen. Press **d** to delete the message and read the next one.

How to Use elm to Send Mail

You can send mail in two ways: from the Unix command line or from the index window. The result is the same with both methods.

To send mail from the command line, give the recipient's address as the argument, as in:

```
% elm jerry@ice.nine.org
```

You can also use the command line to send a file (with no editing) to someone. For instance, to send the file named **setlist,** you would use the command:

```
% elm jerry@ice.nine.org <setlist
```

To send mail from the index window, press **m**. You are then prompted for the address, subject, and so on.

How to Use Commands in the Index Window

elm has many commands for mail handling. They are listed in Table 2.4, with the most common commands listed first.

Table 2.4: elm commands in the index windo

Command	Description
Return, Space	Display the selected message
j, n, ↓	Advance to next undeleted message
J	Advance to next message regardless of status
k, ↑	Go back to previous undeleted message
K	Go back to previous message, regardless of status
+, →	Display next index page
−, ←	Display previous index page
=	Select the first message
*	Select the last message
number	Select the specified message number
d	Delete the selected message
u	Undelete the selected message
r	Reply to just the author of the message

Table 2.4: elm commands in the index window (continued)

Command	Description
g	Reply to all recipients of the message, note that this might send mail to many people
f	Forward the selected message
m	Create a new mail message
s	Save the selected message or tagged messages to a folder
q	Quit with prompts
Q	Quick quit, no prompting
x, Ctrl-Q	Exit leaving folder untouched, ask permission if folder changed
X	Exit leaving folder untouched, unconditionally
t	Tag the selected message for further operations
a	Switch to alias screen
>	Save the selected message or tagged messages to a folder
C	Copy the selected message or tagged messages to a folder
c	Change to another folder
e	Edit the selected folder
o	Change options
b	Bounce the message (similar to forwarding)
/	Search from/subjects for pattern
//	Search entire message texts for pattern
l	Limit messages by specified criteria
Ctrl-D	Delete messages with a specified pattern
Ctrl-T	Tag messages with a specified pattern
Ctrl-U	Undelete messages with a specified pattern
h	Display headers with message

Table 2.4: elm commands in the index window (continued)

Command	Description
Ctrl-L	Redraw screen
p	Print the message or tagged messages on host computer's printer
!	Shell escape
<	Scan the selected message for calendar entries
$	Resynchronize folder
|	Pipe the selected message or tagged messages to a system command
?	List help about the commands

How to Set elm's Options

The **o** command in the index window takes you to the options window.

The options that are most useful are the following:

- The editor you want to use when creating new mail

- The sorting criteria. This tells **elm** the order in which to display the messages. The sorting choices include subject, status, date sent, date received, sender, and length of message. For any choice, you can sort in ascending or descending order.

- Your full name (this appears in each message)

- The user level. Choosing intermediate or advanced levels shows more choices in the index window.

If you change any of the settings, press > to save those changes to **elm**'s settings file so they will take effect each time you run **elm**.

How to Use Aliases in elm

If you often send letters to the same person or same group of people, you will find **elm**'s alias feature incredibly useful. An alias is a shortcut for a mailing address. For instance, if you regularly mail to sandy@rgb.ivideo.com, you could make an alias of sandy. Aliases are also good for making a single name for a group of people to whom you send the same message, such as a department.

From the index window, press **a**. Use the commands at the bottom of this window to edit the aliases. Table 2.5 lists the commands for this window.

Table 2.5: elm alias commands

Command	Description
j, n, ↓	Advance to next undeleted alias
J	Advance to next alias, regardless of status
k, ↑	Go back to previous undeleted alias
K	Go back to previous alias, regardless of status
+, →	Display next alias page
−, ←	Display previous alias page
=	Select the first alias
*	Select the last alias
number	Select the specified alias number
r, q, i	Return to the index window, prompting whether or not to accept changes
R, Q	Return to the index window without prompting
x	Exit from the alias system without updating the alias database
f	Fully expand the selected alias
Space, Return, v	View the address of the selected alias

Table 2.5: elm alias commands (continued)

Command	Description
n	Make a new alias
a	Add the return address of the last message you read to the alias database
c	Change the selected alias
d	Delete the selected alias
u	Undelete the selected alias
m	Mail a message to the selected alias
t	Tag the selected alias for further operations
$	Resynchronize the alias display, processing the deletions and additions to the alias database
l	Limit the alias list by specified criteria
Ctrl-L	Redraw the screen
/	Search for specified name or alias
Ctrl-D	Delete the selected aliases using a specified search pattern
Ctrl-T	Tag all aliases with a specified search pattern
Ctrl-U	Undelete the aliases with a specified search pattern
?	Help on a specific key, or a summary of alias commands

The **a** command is particularly handy. When someone you want to start regular correspondence with sends you mail, go to the aliases window and give the **a** command. This way, you don't have to type in the person's address, possibly introducing an error. Use the **n** command to create an alias when you have not received mail from the other person.

 **See Also** *Mail*

EMACS

One of the oldest and most notorious full-screen editors for Unix systems is **emacs**. **emacs** isn't exactly an editor: it is really an environment, similar to a Unix shell. You can read your mail, manage your files, and check your Usenet news from within **emacs** using the same user interface. **emacs** is free, so many systems have it.

Unfortunately, **emacs**'s interface is often confusing. This is probably because it was written over 15 years ago by someone who was more concerned with power than with consistency. You can do an incredible number of things in **emacs**, including directory maintenance, mail, and accessing Usenet news, and this makes it an excellent editor/environment for power users. Most other people will be much happier with easier editors.

emacs is already powerful, but it can be made even more powerful by advanced users. It is easy to create *macros*, which are intelligent programs that perform many **emacs** operations with a single command. **emacs** was one of the first editors with such capabilities.

There are too many commands to describe here. However, one command should be mentioned: how to quit in case you accidentally run the program without understanding it. Ctrl-X, followed by Ctrl-C, quits the program. (This gives you an idea of how confusing the rest of the commands are.)

EMAIL

See Mail

EMOTICONS

See Smileys

ENCRYPTION

See Security

ERIC

See Educational Resources Information Center

ETIQUETTE

Every society has rules, or at least understandings, between its members. The Internet, being a very new and diverse society, does not have many actual rules, but it has evolved some general guidelines for etiquette.

Understanding the Internet's etiquette guidelines (sometimes jokingly referred to as *netiquette*) will help you get along with others on the Internet. Of course, different people would list different sets of rules. This list is shorter than most, but it hopefully embodies the general tone that you might find on the Internet.

- Don't assume that because you *can* do something, you *should* do it. There are fewer restrictions on the Internet than the average user might be comfortable with.

- Respect others' privacy. With little security on the Internet, many people already feel a bit violated, and making them feel more so will make the Internet a less friendly place to be.

- When posting to a Usenet group or a mailing list, remember that there may be 100 people who read messages for every person who actually posts them. Think about whether what you are posting is something you would want to be read by a newcomer, your parents, your children, or yourself ten years from now.

- Be considerate of Internet resources. When using anonymous **ftp** or **telnet**, try to avoid busy times on the system so that people with more immediate needs are not shut out. Do as much as you can on your local computer before using Internet resources.

- Take responsibility for what you say so that others will feel obliged to do the same. The Internet offers a great deal of anonymity, but that weakens the social bond between the people using it.

- Remember that there are people on the Internet from all different social backgrounds. A great example of this is that many Americans forget that "freedom of speech" is not the law in most countries. Don't assume that others on the Internet have the same rights and responsibilities as you, and learn from that.

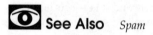 **See Also** *Spam*

EUDORA

One of the most popular mail clients for PCs and Macintosh computers is Eudora by Qualcomm. Eudora has long been considered one of the easiest ways to read, compose, and respond to mail.

Eudora is one of the few graphical programs available that does not require you to have a SLIP or PPP account in order to use it. You can use Eudora with many Unix-based systems that have a standard character-based interface, as long as that system supports the POP protocol, which many do. If you do have a SLIP or PPP account on the Internet, Eudora works particularly well with them.

Figure 2.6 shows how Eudora will appear on your screen. Your mail appears first in your In box, and mail that is waiting to be sent goes in your Out box. You can create as many other boxes as you want. For example, you might want to make one box for your personal correspondence, one for your hobbies, and so on. Of course, all of the windows don't need to be visible at the same time.

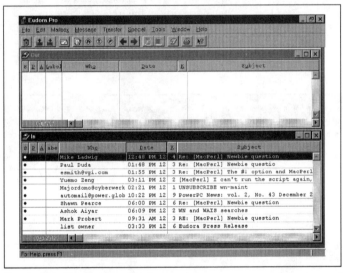

Figure 2.6: Eudora screen

When you receive mail, you can move it from your In box to any of the other boxes very easily. You can even have Eudora move it automatically based on who the mail is from.

There are two editions of Eudora: Eudora Pro, the full-featured commercial version, and Eudora Lite, the freeware version. As you might expect, the commercial edition has many more features and you get better technical support. However, the freeware edition is incredibly popular, and Qualcomm still fixes bugs in that edition.

 **FOR MORE INFORMATION**

Service: **WWW**

URL: `http://www.qualcomm.com/ProdTech/`
                  `quest/`

Description: Use this site to get the latest information
                   on the commercial versions and download
                   the latest copy of the freeware versions.
                   You can also get patches and fixes for both
                   versions here.

EUROPEAN ACADEMIC AND RESEARCH NETWORK

See TERENA

FAQ

See Frequently Asked Questions

FEDERAL NETWORKING COUNCIL

The U.S. federal government is not known for being on the forefront of computer technology, although it has recently shown a great deal more interest in keeping up with network technology. To help coordinate its policies regarding the Internet, the government has recently created the Federal Networking Council, or *FNC*. In its own words,

> "The purpose of the Federal Networking Council (FNC) is to establish an effective interagency forum and long-term strategy to oversee the operation and evolution of the Internet and other national computer networks in support of research and education."

The FNC is only open to federal departments. There are advisory committees that have members of the commercial sector and the public on them. In the future, the FNC will probably have a much larger role in the NII (National Information Infrastructure) since the U.S. government will be a major user of the Internet for regular communications.

FEDERAL DOCUMENTS

See U.S. Government Documents

FIDONET

Before the Internet was easily accessible, bulletin board systems were the most popular means of free-form computer communications.

There were bulletin board systems everywhere, and people loved them. However, there was very little communication between systems. FidoNet was created to tie together the bulletin board community. There are over 20,000 bulletin board systems on FidoNet, and the number is growing by more than 30% each year.

Any BBS that participates on FidoNet can route mail to any other FidoNet site. In addition, the echomail feature allows what used to be local discussion topics to include anyone on the FidoNet. Like the Internet, FidoNet lets people from all over the world communicate easily; unlike the Internet, most FidoNet users do not pay for the service, or pay a much smaller amount than those accessing the Internet.

How to Find a FidoNet Address

Determining an address to send mail to on FidoNet is tricky. You must know the person's login name (which may be one or two names), and the FidoNet address of the person's system. FidoNet addresses are given as $x:yy/zzz.d$, where each part is a number (some addresses do not have the $.d$ part). To form an address, reverse the numbers and precede them with various letters. The example below helps clarify this confusing concept.

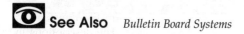 **EXAMPLE**

Assume you want to send mail to "Sarah Billings" on a FidoNet computer with the address $1:394/2.5$. Her mail address from the Internet would be

```
sarah.billings@p5.f2.n394.z1.fidonet.org
```

Or, if you want to send mail to "Knight" at $1:204/0$, the address would be

```
Knight@f0.n204.z1.fidonet.org
```

See Also   *Bulletin Board Systems*

FILE NAMES

See Unix

FILE TRANSFERS

Many people who use the Internet do not have direct connections to it. Instead, they use personal computers and modems at their offices or homes to dial into a host computer. Because most Internet gateways use character-based interfaces, you can use almost any telecommunications program that runs on the personal computer to access the Internet.

What if you want to get files from the Internet, (called *downloading*) or to send a file to your Internet host computer (*uploading*)? These actions are easy to do, but there is no standard way to do them.

There are two types of files that you might want to download or upload: text files (also called *ASCII files*) and binary files. The difference between the two is that text files contain only readable text; binary files contain characters that cannot be read by people. The way that you transfer text files between a personal computer and a Unix host computer is very different from the way you transfer binary files. To complicate matters further, the way that you transfer text and binary files between two Unix computers is also different.

This section describes the Unix commands that you use to transfer files to personal computers. Because there are many kinds of personal computers, and because each type of computer has dozens of kinds of communications software, there are no specific instructions for how to perform the transfers. However, most modern personal computer communications software programs have a few features in common that allow you to perform file transfers, so those features are described in general here. The descriptions in

these sections assume that you are using personal computer software that is reasonably sophisticated; there are plenty of free and
inexpensive programs that will also work just fine.

How to Send Text Files to a Unix Host

The best way to transmit a file from your personal computer to the
Unix host is to have your personal computer "type" the file into a
file on the Unix host. Follow these steps:

1.   On the Unix host, give the **cat** command followed by a >
and the name that you want the text file to be called on
the Unix host. For instance, if you want the file to be
called **sources-list.txt,** you would give the command

```
% cat >sources-list.txt
```

The **cat** command will wait for you to type text into
the file.

2.   On your personal computer, give whatever command is
used to "type" text files on the remote computer. This command's name will often have the word *type* in it or the
words *send text file* or *download text.*

3.   When the file has been typed, press Ctrl-D on the Unix
host. This finishes the file, and you should see the Unix
prompt again.

 NOTE

Do not use any command that has the words *XMODEM,*
YMODEM, ZMODEM, or *Kermit* in them when giving the command to type into the host computer. This will cause the file to become unusable.

How to Get Text Files from a Unix Host

The best method for getting short text files is to use your personal
computer's "capture," "save text," or "upload text" feature, if it has

one. Most programs have such a feature, although it often limits the size of the file you can save. Use the following steps:

1. On the Unix host, type the cat command followed by a < and the name of the file you want to transfer. Do not press ↵ yet.

2. On your personal computer, start the capture, save text, or upload text feature.

3. On the Unix host, press ↵ to start the file transmission.

4. After the file is finished, use whatever feature on your personal computer stops the capturing of the text.

 NOTE

This method does not make an exact copy of the file on your personal computer. The uploaded file will have an extra carriage return character as the first character of the file, and will have the Unix prompt at the end of the file. You can edit out these characters using a text editor, if you wish.

How to Send Binary Files to a Unix Host

In order to send binary files, both computers must be running file transfer software that uses the same transfer protocol. The four most common protocols are XMODEM, YMODEM, ZMODEM, and Kermit. The first three protocols are related: XMODEM was written first and was later superseded by YMODEM, which was followed by ZMODEM. Kermit was written and developed separately. If you have a choice, use ZMODEM, because it is faster and is usually easier.

The most common commands for the protocols are the following:

Protocol	Command
XMODEM	**rx** *filename*
YMODEM	**rb**
ZMODEM	**rz**
Kermit	**kermit -r**

However, there may be different commands on your Unix host; ask your system administrator.

Use these steps to send a file to a Unix host:

1. On the Unix host, give the command that prepares it to receive a file. That command depends on the type of software available on your Unix system, as described above.

2. On your personal computer, use the command that sends binary files. The words *upload*, *transmit binary*, or *send binary* are often in the command name.

3. Hopefully, your personal computer will tell you that the file is being transmitted. It should also tell you when the transmission is finished.

4. If you do not see the Unix prompt on your screen, press ↵ a few times.

As you can tell, these steps don't always work. The most common error is to use mismatched commands on the two computers, as when you try to receive using XMODEM but send with ZMODEM.

Because text files are a subset of binary files, you can send text files as if they were binary files. There are advantages and disadvantages to sending text files as binary files. The advantage is that sending binary files is less susceptible to transmission errors. Because binary file transmission programs assure absolute integrity, you will not be affected by things like phone line noise. The disadvantage is that the format of the text file may not match what is expected by Unix. This is usually only true for file transfers from PC-compatible computers. In Unix text files, each line ends with a carriage return character; in PC text files, lines end with a carriage return character followed by a linefeed character. Unix computers and other personal computers have difficulty reading these kinds of text files.

In order to send text files as binary files, you must be sure that the lines only end with a carriage return character. You should probably try a test file first. After transmission, check the results by displaying the file on the Unix host using the **more** command.

 **EXAMPLE**

Figure 2.7 shows a typical screen as a file is being sent to a Unix host. Here, the PC is running the HyperTerminal program that comes with Windows 95 using the ZMODEM protocol, and the remote Unix host is receiving the file using the **rz** command.

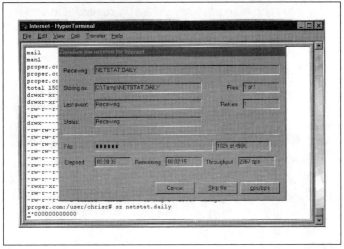

Figure 2.7: Sending a binary file to a Unix host

How to Get Binary Files from a Unix Host

Transferring files from a Unix host to your PC is the reverse of the steps above. The most common commands for the protocols are the following:

Protocol	Command
XMODEM	**sx** *filename*
YMODEM	**sb** *filename*
ZMODEM	**sz** *filename*
Kermit	**kermit -s** *filename*

Again, there may be different commands on your Unix host; ask your system administrator.

These are the steps you need to follow to receive a file from a Unix host:

1. On the Unix host, give the command to start sending files. That command varies with the type of software available on your Unix system, as described above.

2. On your personal computer, use the command to start receiving binary files. You may not need to give any command if you are using the ZMODEM or Kermit protocols; some software detects that a file is being sent in these protocols and starts receiving it automatically.

3. Hopefully, your personal computer will tell you that the file is being transmitted. It should also tell you when the transmission is finished.

4. If you do not see the Unix prompt on your screen, press ↵ a few times.

The same warning given above applies to text files. If you are on a PC-compatible computer, you may or may not be able to read text files transmitted as binary files. The best way to find out is to try a short test file.

e.g. EXAMPLE

Figure 2.8 shows a typical screen as a file is being received from a Unix host. Again, the PC is running the HyperTerminal program that comes with Windows 95 using the ZMODEM protocol, and the remote Unix host is sending the file using the **sz** command.

How to Transfer Files between Unix Computers

If both Unix systems have persistent connections to the Internet, transferring files is fairly easy using the **ftp** command. (The steps for doing this are described in the **ftp** entry of this book.) **ftp** is the only method

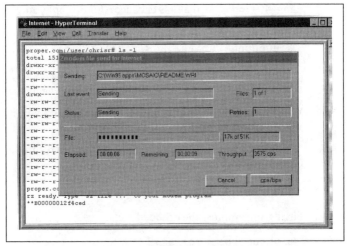

Figure 2.8: Receiving a binary file from a Unix host

you can use to copy files directly; if you can't use the **ftp** command to send a file from the local computer to the remote one, the next best way is to mail the file to someone on the remote computer.

The method you use to mail files depends on the mail program you use. However, regardless of the mail program, it is very important to remember that you cannot mail binary files, only ASCII files. If the file you wanted to transfer is a binary file, use the following steps to convert it to an ASCII file that is compressed. These steps work well for files that are already ASCII files, and will generally make them smaller.

1. Make the file smaller with the **compress** command. The result will be a binary file with the same name as the original but with .Z at the end. For example, if the file you want to send is called spiral, you would use the command

```
% compress spiral
```

2. Use the **uuencode** command to make the compressed binary file a text file. It is a good idea to give the new file a

name that indicates that it is encoded, (for example, adding .uue to the end), as in

```
% uuencode spiral.Z <spiral.Z
  >spiral.Z.uue
```

3. Use your mailing program to send the resulting file.

4. When the recipient gets the file, that person should save it
to the disk on the remote system.

5. To turn it back into a compressed binary file, use the **uudecode** command:

```
% uudecode spiral.Z.uue
```

6. Finally, uncompress the decoded file:

```
% uncompress spiral.Z
```

This will replace the compressed file with the original file.

👁 **See Also**   *ASCII, compress, ftp, Mail, ncftp, uuencode*

FINDING PEOPLE

See Addresses, Mail

FINGER

You can use the **finger** command to check whether or not the login
and host name at a particular site match those of a person you are
looking for. If the person has a login on that computer, and if that

computer responds to **finger** commands, you will get back some valuable information about the user.

The **finger** command is a way to check whether or not someone is on a system without sending them mail. For example, you may want to know whether `lisat@psych.small.edu` is the Lisa Thomas you think teaches there. If you send mail, you have no way of knowing whether the person was your Lisa or just someone with a similar name. If you use the **finger** command, you can probably get back the information you need without contacting the person directly.

Because the **finger** command has been abused in the past, some Internet host computers do not answer requests from outside their systems; some do not support the command even for those on the same system. Usually, you will get a message if this is the case, but you may simply get no reply.

The output of the **finger** command is basic information about the person, plus the information contained in one or two optional files. These files, called .plan and .project, are files that you can put in your directory if you want to give more information on yourself (some systems only support a .plan file). For example, you might give your full name and tell a little about yourself, so that people looking for you can be sure they have the right person. On the other hand, remember that anyone on the Internet can look at your .plan file if your system supports remote **finger** service, so don't give too much personal information.

To find information about someone, use the **finger** command with the person's mailing address as the argument.

 **EXAMPLE**

To see information about `lisat@psych.small.edu`, you would give this command:

```
% finger lisat@psych.small.edu
Login name: lisat   In real life: Lisa Thomas
Office: Kline #112C Office phone: 318-5924
Directory: /usr/bin/lisat
Last login Tue Jan  4 10:52 (PST) on ttyp3
```

```
Plan:
I am Dr. Lisa Thomas, adjunct professor of
psychology at Small University for this
academic year. If I am not available in my
office, please leave a message for me with
the department secretary at extension 5946.
```

How to Use finger for Other Purposes

Some people use their .plan files to do more than identify themselves. Because you can put anything you want in the file, you can use it as a way of broadcasting information to anyone who uses the **finger** command. For instance, some people have sports scores automatically logged into the .plan files so their friends can check the scores easily.

 **EXAMPLE**

You can see the latest news from NASA with the command

```
% finger nasanews@space.mit.edu
```

 **See Also**   *Addresses, Mail*

FIREWALLS

Security on the Internet is clearly a vital topic of interest to many people. There are many types of security that can be implemented, but one of the most effective is a hardware and software combination known as a firewall. Basically, a firewall protects a network from many well-known security attacks coming in from the Internet.

A firewall acts as a gateway through which all Internet traffic going to a network moves. On that gateway is software that checks all the incoming and outgoing messages looking for anything that might be dangerous. Without assuming that a message is or is not danger-ous, the firewall routes the messages to a safe area which is easy to monitor.

Most firewall software makes using Internet services a bit more dif-ficult for people on the network behind the firewall. However, if the firewall is set up properly, those people's data is much safer than if the firewall didn't exist. Thus, the tradeoff of security for convenience is often considered a good one.

 **See Also**   *security*

FIRST VIRTUAL

See Online Commerce

FLAME

The Internet allows anonymous communication. Because you rarely know more than a few of the people with whom you are con-versing, the social rules are very different than in everyday life. This is initially disconcerting for some, but most people get used to it and treat other Internet users with the same respect they would give neighbors and colleagues. However, some people use the ano-nymity of the Internet as an excuse to treat other users unfairly.

When someone lashes out rudely during a discussion on the Internet, it is commonly referred to as *flaming*. This term derives from the derogatory slang phrase that describes someone who is often belligerent or ornery. An interesting derivation of flame is also used in some circles: If you are about to start a harangue, you preface it with "flame on", say your piece, and follow it with "flame off". That's a warning to others that you know you are flaming but want to do it anyway (as compared to many people who do it all the time without being aware of it). Readers of the popular "Fantastic Four" comic books might recognize the derivation of these phrases.

 **See Also**   *Etiquette*

FNC

See Federal Networking Council

FREDMAIL

FrEdMail is another grassroots K-12 education project started in the mid-1980's before easy Internet access was available. FrEdMail allows students and teachers to send each other mail using a network of bulletin board systems. It was written to work on Apple II computers, which are still very popular in many schools. Because the nodes on the network are owned by the schools, they are not required to use outside services to participate.

FrEdMail is free, and it is primarily designed to get kids to write and research collaboratively. Students learn to cooperate on writing papers (for example, collecting science data from different parts of the country) and get a wider audience for the things that they have written. FrEdMail is now linked with the Internet and other networks.

➡️ FOR MORE INFORMATION

Service:	**Mail**
Address:	`help@cerf.net`
Subject:	*Any subject*
Message:	*Any request for information on FrEdMail*
Description:	CERFnet supports the gateway between FrEdMail and the Internet and has helped the non-profit FrEdMail Foundation.

FREE-NETS

Many bulletin board systems charge users for using the system or for certain privileges. This helps support the large systems, but it excludes many people from being able to use them. Free-Nets™ are bulletin board systems that are always free and specialize in giving community computer access. Free-Nets are organized by the National Public Telecomputing Network (NPTN), a group that wants to be to computers what National Public Radio and Public Broadcasting System are to radio and television.

The basic idea is that people and businesses in every community should have access to network services such as bulletin boards and electronic mail, even if they cannot afford to pay for them. To use a Free-Net, all you need is a modem and a terminal or personal computer. Many Free-Nets are used for community organization, education, and distribution of information.

Most of the existing Free-Nets are connected to the Internet. It should be emphasized that Free-Nets do not exist only as a free way of getting on the Internet: their local community aspect is more important. A few Free-Nets are for K-12 school access only.

 **FOR MORE INFORMATION**

Service:	**WWW**
URL:	`http://www.nptn.org/`
Description:	Information about current Free-Nets and how to help set up a new Free-Net.

FREEWARE

See archives

FREQUENTLY ASKED QUESTIONS

As new users start reading Usenet news groups, they often ask the same questions over and over. To prevent the same introductory questions from repeatedly appearing, many of the groups have created files called Frequently Asked Questions, or *FAQs*. FAQs are often organized by one person with the input of many others, and are a great example of the volunteerism that has helped the Internet grow.

When you join a Usenet news group, you should see if there is a FAQ for the group. It is not always easy to find the FAQs in the groups, but there are places that all known FAQs are stored, so you can look there (see below). Even if you don't intend to read a particular news group, you might find the FAQ associated with the group to be an interesting introduction to the subject.

FAQs can also be found in a set of Usenet news groups specifically set up for them. These groups have the name (*.answers*) at the end of their title. Although not all people who write FAQs put them in these groups, many do. Generally, every FAQ is posted to the news.answers group. Most FAQs are also posted to the .answers group for the news hierarchy they are in.

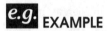 **EXAMPLE**

To find information on tattooing and body piercing, look in the rec.arts.bodyart news group for a posting that looks like a FAQ. You can also look in news.answers and rec.answers for the same files.

 **FOR MORE INFORMATION**

Service:	**Anonymous ftp**
Host:	`rtfm.mit.edu`
Location:	/pub/usenet
Description:	This is the top level of a hierarchy that matches that of the Usenet news. Each news group has its own directory, and all the FAQ files for that news group are in the directory. There are many sites that have duplicates of the information at rtfm.mit.edu; one such site is ftp.uu.net.

⊙ **See Also** *Lists of Lists, Usenet News*

FTP

One of the most popular features of the Internet is the ability to get files from other computers. This feature alone was one of the main reasons that the Internet grew so quickly in its early years. Groups of researchers around the world could share data simply by putting it on one computer and then individually downloading it to their computers when they wanted to. The basic program to transfer files between Unix computers is **ftp**. (Some Internet hosts do not support **ftp** because they do not have persistent connections.)

ftp has been around for a long time, and its unfriendly interface shows it. Most people prefer **ncftp**, an improved version of **ftp** that can take the same commands, but has many interface improvements. Some **ftp** sites also support the gopher program, which is much friendlier and easier to use than **ftp**. You should get familiar with both ncftp and gopher before deciding that **ftp** is the only way to do file transfers. There are also many FTP client programs for Windows and the Macintosh. Figure 2.9 shows a typical graphical FTP client.

ftp is most commonly used to copy files from a remote system to your local Unix host. Once the files are there, you can read them, edit them, pass them along, transfer them to your personal computer, and so on. In this case, **ftp** is mostly used for copying from central repositories. The commands for doing this are described below.

A less common use for **ftp** is to copy files from your local Unix host to a remote site. For example, you may want to share a file with others, and the best way to transfer it is with **ftp**. Because these commands are used less often, they are described separately below.

Using **ftp** can sometimes be confusing to beginners who don't understand what is happening on each computer. In the description below, *local computer* is the Unix host that you have an account on and *remote computer* is the computer to which you are connecting. Keep in mind that there are directories on each computer. You will get a file or files from a directory on the remote computer and possibly copy them to a directory on the local computer (probably in your home directory).

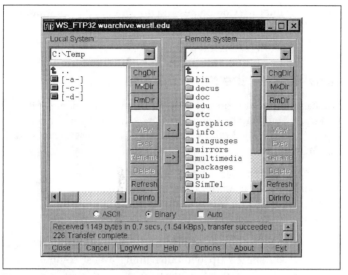

Figure 2.9: FTP client for Windows

How to Use Anonymous ftp

When you connect to another computer with **ftp**, you must give an account name and password. This is a common security precaution. However, many sites want anyone to be able to get files from them without having to know a special account name and password. A standard has been adopted by most sites that allow such access: you always use *anonymous* as the account name and your mailing address as the password. This method is called *anonymous ftp* and has become a widespread standard. There are more than a thousand sites that allow anonymous **ftp**. Usually, when you log in as *anonymous*, the remote system only gives you access to a restricted set of files.

Because there are so many places that allow anonymous **ftp**, searching for files can be quite difficult. The **archie** command, described earlier in this book, is an excellent way to find the files you want among the many sites.

When you use the **ftp** command, you open a link on the remote computer. This action uses resources both on the remote computer and on the Internet. Companies and universities that allow anonymous **ftp** usually do so as a public service, so you should respect the service and not stay connected longer than necessary.

How to Give the ftp Command

You can give the **ftp** command by itself or with the name of the remote host you want to connect to. For example, if you are connecting to the host called `wuarchive.wustl.edu`, use the following command:

```
% ftp wuarchive.wustl.edu
Connected to wuarchive.wustl.edu.
220 wuarchive.wustl.edu FTP server ready.
Name (wuarchive.wustl.edu:chrisr):
```

ftp's prompt is simply ftp>. Give commands to this prompt. For example, if you started **ftp** without naming a host computer, you would open the host with the **open** command, as in

```
% ftp
ftp> open wuarchive.wustl.edu
Connected to wuarchive.wustl.edu.
220 wuarchive.wustl.edu FTP server ready.
Name (wuarchive.wustl.edu:chrisr):
```

In each case, the remote computer is asking for your user name; enter **anonymous**:

```
Name (wuarchive.wustl.edu:chrisr): anonymous
331 Guest login ok, send ident as password.
Password:
```

Next, type in your mailing address. Most anonymous **ftp** computers will accept any characters for the password, but it is polite to tell them who you are in case they are keeping statistics.

```
Password: chrisr@english.small.edu
230 Guest login ok, access restrictions
 apply.
ftp>
```

You will not see your mailing address as you type it. You are now at **ftp**'s prompt.

 NOTE

You may not be able to log in on your first attempt. There may be many other people also trying to download files, and the remote computer's operator might have set a limit to how many people can access the files. You might see a message such as

```
530 Too many users connected currently.
  Please try again later.
```

Try again later, preferably during a non-peak time.

Commands for Receiving Files

Once you have started **ftp**, you can start giving commands. Common **ftp** commands are shown in Table 2.6. The commands are listed beginning with the most commonly used.

Table 2.6: ftp commands for receiving files

Command	Description
open *host*	Starts a connection with the named host
close	Closes the current connection and returns to **ftp**'s prompt
disconnect	Same as the **close** command
bye	Closes the current connection and returns to Unix
quit	Same as the **bye** command
cd *remote-directory*	Changes the directory on the remote machine
cdup	Changes to the directory above on the remote host; this is the same as the **cd ..** command.

Table 2.6: ftp commands for receiving files (continued)

Command	Description
pwd	Tells you the name of the current directory
dir	Lists the long contents of the directory, similar to the Unix command **ls -l**. You can also specify the directory to list, such as **dir /pub**.
ls	Lists the short contents of the directory, similar to the Unix command **ls**. You can also specify the directory to list, such as **ls /pub**.
get *remote-file*	Copies the named file from the remote host and stores it in the current directory on the local host with the same file name. You can also give a second argument, *local-file*, if you want to store the file with a different file name.
mget *remote-files*	Like the **get** command, but gets more than one file. It is common to use this command with wildcard characters like "*".
prompt	Turns prompting on and off. Normally, the **mget** command prompts you for each file to be sure you want to copy it. If you give the **prompt** command to turn off prompting, the files are copied automatically.
ascii	Specifies that the files you are transferring are ASCII files. This mode is a tiny bit faster than binary mode, but will not work if the file you are transferring is not truly ASCII. ASCII mode is the default.

Table 2.6: ftp commands for receiving files (continued)

Command	Description
binary	Specifies that the files you are transferring are binary files. This mode is a little slower than ASCII mode, but is safer.
lcd *local-directory*	Changes the directory on your local host (for example, if you want to put the files you are about to get in a different place). If you don't include the directory name, you are changed to your home directory.
bell	Causes a beep on your personal computer for each file that is received
runique	Turns off and on file renaming when you get files that have the same name as files on your local host. Normally, if you get a file that already exists, the new file will replace the file on the disk of the local host. Giving the **runique** command causes **ftp** to add a *.1*, *.2*, and so on to the end of the duplicate file name.
hash	Causes a # to appear for each block of data that is transferred.
status	Displays information about all of **ftp**'s current settings.
$ *macro-name*	Runs the macro
help	Displays help. You can include the name of the **ftp** command for which you want help.
?	Same as the **help** command

As you saw earlier, the **open** command lets you establish a connection with a remote host. This is useful after using the **close** command: you don't have to leave the **ftp** program if you want to switch to a different host. If you do want to quit, use the **bye** or **quit** commands.

After you are connected to a remote host, you can move around the host's directory tree using the **cd** and **cdup** commands. To see which directory you are in, use the **pwd** command. The **dir** and **ls** commands tell you what files are in the directory.

If you find a file that you want to copy to your local host, use the **get** command. For example, many directories on anonymous **ftp** servers have files with names like README that describe the contents of the directory. If you want to get that file, give the command get README.

If you want more than one file, use the **mget** command. For instance, to get all the files in a directory, you would give the command `mget*`

Notice that the **mget** command prompts you for each file that you might download. This can be tedious. Before giving the **mget** command, give the **prompt** command to turn off **ftp**'s prompt mode.

ftp's default assumes that the files you are downloading are in ASCII format. If you are downloading binary files, it is absolutely necessary to give the **binary** command before doing so. If you don't, the files will be corrupted in the transfer. Use the **ascii** command to switch back to ASCII mode.

ftp normally puts the files in the current directory on the local host. You can change this in two ways. The easiest method is to change the current directory on the local host with the **lcd** command:

```
ftp> lcd internet-files
Local directory now /u3/chrisr/internet-files
ftp>
```

If you are transferring many files and want to hear when each one is finished, use the **bell** command. The **hash** command causes **ftp** to type a # on the screen as the file is being transferred, so you can watch its progress. The **runique** command is also useful if you are not sure whether or not files with the same name already exist in your directory on the local host. To see how all of **ftp**'s options are set, use the **status** command:

```
ftp> status
Connected to netcom.com.
No proxy connection.
```

```
Mode: stream; Type: ascii; Form: non-print;
Structure: file Verbose: on; Bell: off;
Prompting: on; Globbing: on
Store unique: off; Receive unique: off
Case: off; CR stripping: on
Ntrans: off
Nmap: off
Hash mark printing: on; Use of PORT cmds: on
ftp>
```

Commands for Sending Files

Some remote hosts allow you to send files to them using **ftp**. This is rarely the case if you connect through anonymous **ftp**, because doing so would be a security risk. However, you can often connect with a host using a specified login and password. Table 2.7 shows the additional commands for sending files to a remote host. Notice that they are very similar to the commands you have already seen, but with the direction of the transfer reversed.

Table 2.7: ftp commands for sending files

Command	Description
put *local-file*	Copies the named file from your local host and stores it with the same file name in the current directory on the remote host. You can also give a second argument, *remote-file*, if you want to store the file with a different file name.
send	Same as the **put** command
mput local-files	Like the **put** command, but sends more than one file. It is common to use this command with wildcard characters like *.
append *local-file* *remote-file*	Appends the contents of the local file to the end of the remote file.
rename *from to*	Renames the file on the remote host

Table 2.7: ftp commands for sending files (continued)

Command	Description
delete *remote-file*	Deletes the file from the remote host
mdelete *remote-files*	Like the **delete** command, but deletes more than one file. It is common to use this command with wildcard characters like *.
mkdir *remote-directory-name*	Makes a new directory on the remote host.
rmdir *remote-directory-name*	Removes a directory from the remote host.
sunique	Turns off and on file renaming when you send files that have the same name as files that already exist on the remote host. Normally, if you send a file that already exists, the new file will replace the file on the remote host. Giving the **sunique** command causes **ftp** to add a *.1*, *.2*, and so on to the end of the duplicate file name.

The **put** and **mput** commands are the main commands you will use to send files. If you are simply adding the contents of a local file to the end of a remote file (for example, adding comments to the end of a growing discussion), use the **append** command. You can perform other file and directory maintenance with **ftp** using the **rename**, **delete**, **mdelete**, **mkdir**, and **rmdir** commands.

For example, assume that you want to put the file called new-material in the current directory of the remote host:

```
ftp> put new-material
200 PORT command successful.
150 ASCII data connection for new-material
226 ASCII Transfer complete.
local: new-material remote: new-material
646 bytes sent in 0.041 seconds (15 Kbytes/s)
ftp>
```

How to Use the .netrc File

When you start **ftp** using a host name, the command looks for a file called .netrc in your home directory. You can put commands in that file to make connecting to hosts with **ftp** more automatic. For each system you normally connect to with **ftp**, you can have an entry that passes your login name (such as *anonymous*) and password to the system. You can also define macros, which are sets of **ftp** commands that are automatically executed.

An example of a .netrc file might be

```
machine wuarchive.wustl.edu
        login anonymous
        password chrisr@english.small.edu

machine rtfm.mit.edu
        login anonymous
        password chrisr@english.small.edu
        macdef init
        cd /pub/usenet-by-hierarchy
        prompt
        hash
```

Each entry starts with the word *machine* and the name of the remote host. If you open that remote host, **ftp** looks for a line with the words *login* and/or *password* and uses those to log you in automatically. In the example file, if you open wuarchive.wustl.edu, **ftp** will open the connection with an anonymous login for you.

Note that the .netrc file must not have read or write permissions for anyone other than yourself. See the "Security" entry for information on permissions.

The second part of the example file shows an *init macro*. Macros are an advanced feature that can save you typing. The lines after the words *macdef init* are automatically executed after a successful login. In this case, you automatically change to the /pub/usenet-by-hierarchy directory, and the **prompt** and **hash** commands are given.

You can also create other macros to execute as you run **ftp**. For example, if you often switch to the directory /pub/usenet-by-group, you could add a macro to your .netrc file, instead of having to give the **cd** command every time:

```
macdef grp
cd /pub/usenet-by-group
```

When you run **ftp**, you simply give the command **$grp**, and the macro runs, saving you a great deal of typing.

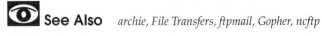 **See Also**   *archie, File Transfers, ftpmail, Gopher, ncftp*

FTPMAIL

If the Internet host you use does not support **ftp**, you can still get files from anonymous **ftp** sites using ftpmail. Send a letter to a system supported by Digital Equipment Corporation (DEC) with instructions on how to get the files you want, and that machine retrieves the files and sends them back to you by mail. This is much less convenient than having real **ftp** access, but it works well for those people who don't have such access.

To use ftpmail, send mail to **ftpmail@decwrl.dec.com,** with a blank subject. In the message, give specific commands for the host you want to open, the directory in which the file resides, and the file or files you want. You can also use ftpmail to get a directory from a host so you can later ask for files.

The commands, which are similar to those in **ftp**, are as follows:

Command	Description
connect *host*	Name of the host that has the files
chdir *directory*	Location of the file or files you want
get *file*	Retrieves the file

Command	Description
ls *directory*	Return a directory listing instead of a file
ascii	Use ASCII mode for transfer (this is the default)
binary	Use binary mode for transfer
compress	Compress the output using the **compress** command
uuencode	Convert binary data to text using the **uuencode** command
btoa	Convert binary data to text using the **btoa** command
chunksize *size*	Limit the mail that comes back to the number of characters specified; the default is 64,000
quit	The last command in your letter

When you send the letter, you can use any subject line you want; that subject line will be in the subject of the letter you get back with the file so that you can track your requests. You can ask for up to ten files in a single message.

You will quickly receive a reply—this is not your file. The reply tells you what you sent and where your request is in the queue. The reply also verifies that the host you specified in the connect command was valid. The file should arrive within a day or two, sometimes less, depending on how many files are being requested by others and how busy the mail system is (files are sent at lowest priority).

A common problem with ftpmail is that the message that comes back is too long. Some systems, particularly commercial networks, restrict the length of letters that you can receive. Use the **chunksize** command in the letter to set the maximum size of the message. If the file you request is longer than the specified chunksize, the file will be split over multiple messages. Unsplitting the file may be difficult, depending on your host system.

e.g. EXAMPLE

To get a copy of the complete *Americans with Disabilities Act*, create a letter with the following commands:

```
connect handicap.shel.isc-br.com
binary
uuencode
chdir /pub/ada
get ADA726.ZIP
quit
```

To get a listing of all the files in that directory, you would instead use these commands:

```
connect handicap.shel.isc-br.com
chdir /pub/ada
ls
quit
```

FOR MORE INFORMATION

Service:	**Mail**
Address:	ftpmail@decwrl.dec.com
Subject:	*Any subject line*
Message:	help
Description:	Sends back a complete list of commands and some tips on using ftpmail.

 **See Also** *ftp*

FYI

Many of the standardized documents on the Internet are quite technical. The main series of these is called *Requests for Comments,* or *RFCs.* A few of the early RFCs were distinctly non-technical, and were therefore put in their own series so that they were easier to find. That series is called the FYIs, short for "For Your Information."

The FYI notes are meant to be useful to anyone who has questions about the Internet. Some cover common questions about how to do things, others cover organizations with Internet-related purposes, and so on.

These are the current FYI papers (new ones are constantly being added):

Number	Title
1	F.Y.I. on F.Y.I.: Introduction to the F.Y.I. notes
2	FYI on a network management tool catalog: Tools for monitoring and debugging TCP/IP internets and interconnected devices
3	FYI on where to start: A bibliography of internetworking information
4	FYI on questions and answers: Answers to commonly asked "new Internet user" questions
5	Choosing a name for your computer
6	FYI on the X window system
7	FYI on Questions and Answers: Answers to commonly asked "experienced Internet user" questions
8	Site Security Handbook
9	Who's who in the Internet: Biographies of IAB, IESG, and IRSG members

Number	Title
10	There's Gold in them thar Networks! or Searching for Treasure in all the Wrong Places
11	Catalog of Available X.500 Implementations
12	Building a network information services infrastructure
13	Executive introduction to directory services using the X.500 protocol
14	Technical overview of directory services using the X.500 protocol
15	Privacy and accuracy issues in network information center databases
16	Connecting to the Internet: What connecting institutions should anticipate
17	The Tao of IETF: A Guide for New Attendees of the Internet Engineering Task Force
18	Internet Users' Glossary
19	Introducing the Internet
20	What Is the Internet
21	A survey of Advanced Uses of X.500
22	Answers to commonly asked "Primary and Secondary School Internet User" questions
23	Guide to network resource tools
24	How to use anonymous FTP
25	Status report on networked information retrieval: tools and groups
26	K-12 internetworking guidelines
27	Tools for DNS debugging
28	Netiquette guidelines

FOR MORE INFORMATION

Service:	**Anonymous ftp**
Host:	`ds.internic.net`
Path:	/fyi
Description:	This directory has all the FYIs available as well as an index to them.

👁 **See Also**   *Request For Comments, STD*

GAMES

Many people use the Internet for recreation, and there are many network-related games available. Unfortunately, many of the hosts on which these run come and go. At various times, there have been servers for backgammon, go, chess, poker, Diplomacy, and other common board and card games. There are other servers for some games that not only run on a network, but in fact require a network to play.

Many games that people associate with the Internet are not net-specific. One of the most common examples is Rogue, a single-user fantasy game with dungeons, dragons, and so on. Because it is played on Unix computers and the Internet has many Unix computers that you can run the game on, some people think of Rogue as an "Internet game," but it is not. Many of these types of games are available for free at anonymous **ftp** sites.

There are many Usenet news groups devoted to games. Most are in the rec.games. hierarchy, (for example, in rec.games.backgammon and rec.games.pinball). If you are interested in games, read some of those groups, or at least the FAQs for them. There are also mailing lists for players of various games.

FOR MORE INFORMATION

Service:	**Mailing List**
Name:	The games list
Address:	`listserv@brownvm.brown.edu`
Subject:	*Any subject*
Message:	subscribe games-l *your-name*
Description:	This is a general discussion of computer games.

Service:	**WWW**
URL:	`http://www.gamesdomain.co.uk`
Description:	This is a great resource about games of all sorts. There are lists of FAQs, Usenet news groups, other World Wide Web servers, and so on.

See Also *MUD*

GATEWAY

A gateway is a piece of hardware or software that lets two dissimilar networks communicate. Most of the Internet uses a single communication protocol called *TCP/IP*, and thus no gateways are needed. However, some networks connected to the Internet do not run TCP/IP and must go through a gateway to connect to the Internet. A network using a gateway looks just like any other network to other Internet users; the process of translating through the gateway is transparent.

 **See Also**   *Router*

GEOGRAPHIC NAME SERVERS

See Domain Name System

GIF FILES

There are hundreds of ways to store photographic and artistic images in files, which can make distributing images difficult. An additional problem is that each full-color file can take up a huge amount of disk space. CompuServe created a compact way of storing and distributing images called the *Graphics Interchange Format* (better known as *GIF*), which has been adopted by many networks. There are freeware and shareware programs to display GIF images on virtually every type of computer, and many commercial photography programs have GIF converters built in.

If you come across a file that has *.gif* at the end of its name, you can safely assume that it is a GIF file. When transferring GIF files, do not compress them: they are already internally compressed.

GOPHER

In the past few years, many new tools for searching for information on the Internet have appeared. One that became popular very quickly is Gopher. Gopher is a client/server system that lets you navigate through the Internet without using any confusing commands.

Gopher is a simple menu-driven program that makes finding information much easier than older programs such as **ftp**. Some advantages of using Gopher include the following:

- Directory trees are shown as lists. To choose a file to view or transfer, you do not need to type its name.

- It is easy for a computer site running a Gopher server to use different organization for their files than just the static Unix directories. If you run a Gopher server, you can add parts of the directory tree that do not match any part of your file structure. The entries are plain text, not file names, and are thus easier to read.

- Links can be to files on other computers. This vastly reduces the amount of redundant information on the Internet. For instance, instead of copying some files from another host computer, you set up your Gopher server to automatically access those files on their home server, as if they were resident on your local drive.

- Gopher can link to other services. For example, you can have an entry that automatically starts a link to another computer through the **telnet** program.

- There are Gopher clients for most computer platforms. The one covered in this section is the character-based Unix client simply called **gopher**. However, there are many other graphical clients available.

- Most Gopher clients are customizable. When you find a place that you think you will return to, you store a *bookmark* to that location in your client software so that getting to that location is almost instantaneous.

- Gopher is designed handle any kind of information (text, programs, pictures, etc.). There are experimental versions of the server and clients (which may be available by the time you read this) that handle pictures, sound, MIME data, World Wide Web links, and other types of information.

- Combined with **veronica** (see the "**veronica**" entry for more information), you can quickly search on all known Gopher servers for particular information.

It is important to understand which part of Gopher is the client and which part is the server. The *client* is the software you run on your personal computer or on your local host. You use the client to access Gopher servers elsewhere on the Internet. A Gopher *server* is software that runs on some Internet host computers and points to information. You cannot use your Gopher client to get information from a remote computer that is not running the Gopher server software. In other words, if you want to provide information for other people on the Internet to access using Gopher clients, your local computer must run Gopher server software. World Wide Web client software can also act as Gopher clients.

There are also many Gopher client programs both for Windows and the Macintosh. Figure 2.10 shows a typical graphical Gopher client.

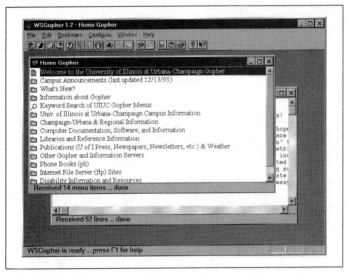

Figure 2.10: Gopher client for Windows

How to Start the Gopher Program

Although each type of Gopher client is a bit different, many look quite similar and have similar features. The Unix **gopher** program is described here because it is one of the most common ways of accessing Gopher information.

To start the program, give the **gopher** command. The initial screen is shown in Figure 2.11. The top line tells you the version of the **gopher** program, and the next line tells you the name of the server to which you are connected. Because you did not specify a server, **gopher** used the default server, at `gopher2.tc.umn.edu`. The numbered lines are the current menu choices.

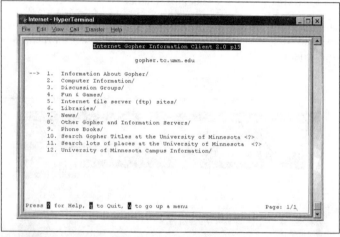

Figure 2.11: Initial **gopher** window

You can also start the **gopher** program using the name of a Gopher server that you want to look at as the argument. For example, to start **gopher** at the server at the Smithsonian Institution's Museum of Natural History, you would give the command

```
% gopher nmnhgoph.si.edu
```

How to Navigate in gopher

Navigating around in *gopherspace* (that is, all the Gopher servers on the Internet) is quite easy. In the **gopher** program, use the ↑ and ↓ keys to move the arrow to the item you want to see and press ↵. You can also choose an item directly by typing its item number and pressing ↵. For example, choose the first option in the menu shown in Figure 2.10, "Information About Gopher/" and press ↵. You see the set of choices shown in Figure 2.12.

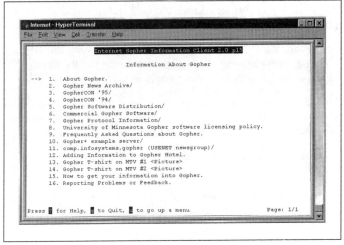

Figure 2.12: Another **gopher** window

The Gopher server gives you hints about what kind of information each choice has. The last characters of each line tell you about what will happen if you select the option. The most likely choices are:

Characters	Description
/	Another menu
.	A text document you can read
<?>	An index you can search

Characters	Description
<picture>	A picture you can view (if your client software supports pictures)
<bin>	A binary file you can download
<tel>	A connection to a **telnet** server
<)	A sound file
<cso>	A campus telephone and address search program

Some Gopher clients let you see pictures and hear sound files. **gopher**, of course, does not because it is character-based.

For instance, if you select item #8 (either by pressing the ↓ key or typing **8**, then pressing ↵), you will see the text of the file that explains common questions about **gopher**.

Files do not go flying by you on the screen: they stop at each page so you can read them at your own pace. When they stop, they display this message at the bottom of the screen:

```
--More--(2%)[Press space to continue, 'q' to
quit.]
```

The number in the parentheses tells you what percentage of the total file you have already seen, so you know how much more there is to read.

gopher normally uses Unix's **more** command to show you pages of text. When you are paging though a text file, you have many options on what to do at the end of each page. The most common is simply to press the Spacebar to see the next page. Another common action is to type **/** and enter text to search for. Typing **?** shows you all of your options.

When you are finished reading the file (or you typed **q** to stop), **gopher** displays your choices for what to do with the file:

```
Press <RETURN> to continue, <m> to mail, <D>
to download, <s> to save, or <p> to print:
```

You have many options:

- If you are through with the file, press ⏎.

- You can mail the file to someone. You are prompted for the mailing address.

- If your personal computer software has XMODEM, YMODEM, ZMODEM, or Kermit capabilities, or can turn on text file capturing, you can download it to your personal computer. You are prompted for the file transfer protocol.

- You can save it as a text file on your local host computer. You can choose the name to give the file.

- If your local host computer allows you to print files (few do), you can print it.

Choosing an entry that ends with a / character takes you to another menu, which may not be on the computer you started on. This is one of Gopher's most powerful features. For example, in the screen shown in Figure 2.12, entry 5, Gopher Software Distribution/, is on the same computer as the menu, but entry 4, "comp.infosystems.gopher (USENET newsgroup)/," is on a different computer in a different state.

People creating Gopher servers make these links to other computers, making your task of moving around in gopherspace as easy as pressing ↑, ↓, and ⏎. Each time you go to a new computer, your link with the old computer is severed, but **gopher** remembers how to get back there, as you will see in the next section.

How to Use gopher's Navigation Commands

So far, you have seen how to use the ↑, ↓, and ⏎ keys, and how to type the number of an entry to move to it. Of course, **gopher** gives you more options than these. The keys are summarized in Table 2.8.

The → key acts the same as the ⏎ key. Pressing ← or **u** takes you back one menu. This makes retreating from your current position easy, so you can be a bit more adventurous as you search. Pressing ← many times will take you all the way back to where you started (typing **m** will get you there immediately).

Table 2.8: gopher keyboard summary

Key	Action
↑	Move to previous line
↓	Move to next line
→, ↵	Go to the selected menu or display the selected item
←, u	Go to previous menu
>, +, PgDn, Spacebar	View next page of menu
<, −, PgUp, b	View previous page of menu
number	Go to the numbered line
m	Go back to the main menu
o	Open a new Gopher server by name
s	Save the selected item to a file
D	Download the selected item using file transfer protocols
/	Search for an item in this menu
n	Find the next search item
a	Add the selected item to the bookmark list
A	Add the current menu to the bookmark list
v	View the bookmark list
d	Delete a bookmark from your list
=	Show internal information about the selected item, such as its location and size
O	Show options menu
!	Start a Unix shell
q	Quit, prompting first
Q	Quit with no prompt

Some menus take up more than one page. You can tell whether this is the case by looking in the lower-right corner of the menu, which shows you the current page number and the total number of pages. To move to the next page of a multi-page menu, press >, +, PgDn, or the Spacebar; to move to the previous page, press <, –, PgUp, or **b**. If you try to move past the end or the beginning of a multi-page menu, **gopher** wraps around as if the menu was a long loop.

You may not always find what you are looking for using the searching keys. If you know the name of a Gopher server that you want to go to directly, type **o** and enter the name. This also prompts you for the *port number*, but that number is almost always 70 for Gopher servers.

When you find items you want to save, you do not need to open them in order to save them. Typing **s** saves the file to disk (with a name you specify), and typing **D** downloads it to your personal computer (assuming your software has XMODEM, YMODEM, ZMODEM, or Kermit capabilities).

On a multi-page menu, you may want to find a particular item quickly. Type **/** and enter the string of characters to search for. Type **n** to repeat that search. This is useful when you have searched with **veronica** and many of the options have similar names.

The **a**, **A**, **v**, and **d** commands let you work with *bookmarks*, which are references to Gopher menus and files. Bookmarks are stored in a file on your local host called .gopherrc. When you find a place that you might want to return to, you can store a reference to that place as a bookmark. Note that typing **a** makes the current selection a bookmark; typing **A** command makes the current menu a bookmark.

You can view your bookmarks menu by typing **v**. After you have created many bookmarks, you may want to start **gopher** with your bookmarks page showing first; to do so, start the program using the –b option:

```
% gopher -b
```

You can remove entries from your bookmark page by typing **d**.

If you want to see where an item resides before you enter that item on a menu, type **=**. You will see something like this:

```
Type=1+
Name=Special Collections: Internet Help
```

```
Path=1/Special Collections: Internet Help
Host=nysernet.org
Port=70
ModDate=Tue Oct 19 11:25:59 1993
  <19931019112559>
```

In this case, you can see the host (nysernet.org), the path to get to the selected item on that host, and so on.

gopher lets you specify which Unix commands get executed when viewing and printing different kinds of files. For example, the default for viewing a text file is Unix's **more** command, but you may have another command (such as a text editor) you want to run instead. You can also specify what commands to use when displaying graphics, playing sounds, and so on. To change these, type **O** in **gopher**, choose the kind of applications (display or printing) you want to change, and enter new commands.

While running **gopher**, you may want to run Unix commands. You can start a Unix shell by typing **!**, then perform the commands and return to **gopher** by giving the Unix **exit** command.

Of course, you will want to leave the **gopher** program at some time. To do so, type **q** or **Q**, or press Ctrl-C.

 **See Also** *ftp, veronica*

GOVERNMENT DOCUMENTS

See U.S. Government documents

GRAPHICS INTERCHANGE FORMAT

See GIF Files

HOME PAGE

The term "home page" has taken on many meanings as the Web has developed. It originally meant the first page that you saw when you went to a particular Web site. It also meant the page that people had set their Web browsers to look at when the browser first ran. As individuals started creating their own Web content, the term started to mean an individual's personal page, or the page that someone has created and uses to advertise to the world.

HTML

The structure of the World Wide Web (also known as *WWW*) is based on text files that have special formatting instructions in them. Those instructions are in *HTML*, which stands for *HyperText Markup Language*. To use the hypertext linking in HTML files, you need a program such as **lynx**, **Mosaic**, or **WWW**. If you learn the rules for adding HTML to text files (and those rules are pretty complicated), you can create your own hypertext documents.

FOR MORE INFORMATION

Service: **WWW**

URL: `http://www.ncsa.uiuc.edu/`
                `demoweb/html-primer.html`

Description: An introduction to how to make HTML
                files. It is a hypertext document that has
                many links to other documents, which are
                good examples for learning about HTML.

See Also   *Hypertext Link, lynx, Netscape*

HTTP

The HyperText Transfer Protocol (HTTP) is the method used to make hypertext documents readable on the World Wide Web. Web servers and clients speak to each other using HTTP, so end users don't need to know anything about its intricacies.

HTTP is a stateless protocol, meaning that the client and the server programs speak to each other only once and that a connection is not retained. A Web client program sends a single request to the Web server for information, and the Web server responds with a single reply. If the client wants to ask the server for more information, it must reestablish the connection.

HYPERTEXT LINK

Web pages have words, phrases, and URL addresses that are set aside from the rest of the text either by being underlined or given a separate font color. These are known as *Hypertext Links*. Hypertext links are direct connections to other sites on the Internet that provide further information. Clicking on the hypertext activates the link and pulls up the chosen site.

 See Also   *HTML, lynx, Mosaic, World Wide Web*

HYTELNET

Many library catalogs and some databases are available only by logging onto a remote computer using the **telnet** program. Unfortunately, **telnet** is not terribly friendly, and its commands are a bit obscure. To alleviate this, Hytelnet was developed as a friendly front-end to **telnet**. Hytelnet lets you choose which computer to log into from a hypertext list of libraries and other systems that allow public **telnet** connections.

To start Hytelnet, give the **hytelnet** command. Use the ↑ and ↓ keys to move the selection up and down in the menus. For menus with multiple pages, use the + and − keys. To get help at any time, type **?**. Type **q** to quit Hytelnet.

The menus in Hytelnet let you explore the kinds of services offered on the Internet. The first choice lists most of the publicly-accessible college library catalogs. The next lets you choose from other Internet sites. Hytelnet is not the solution to all of your problems, however. Once you choose a site to connect to, you must follow the directions for that system. For example, most library card catalog systems have different interfaces and require different commands. Hytelnet can't give you the information you need to learn these systems. On the other hand, having an updated list of all the college library catalogs available in one place is certainly a boon for many researchers that outweighs the confusion about how to use them.

 See Also   *Library Catalogs, telnet*

IAB

See Internet Architecture Board

IETF

See Internet Engineering Task Force

IGC

The Institute for Global Communications is the U.S. branch of an international Internet service provider (APC) dedicated to serving non-governmental organizations and grass-roots activists around the world. Home to PeaceNet, EcoNet, WomensNet, LaborNet, and ConflictNet, igc has a broad user base. They support online conferences ranging from prison issues to organic farming, and provide full Internet access to a multitude of organizations and individuals. Additionally, as a non-profit organization, igc offers reduced rates for underfunded, politically progressive groups.

 FOR MORE INFORMATION

Service:	**WWW**
URL:	`http://www.igc.apc.org`
Description:	Contains information and links to all of igc's networks.

 **See Also**   *EcoNet, PeaceNet*

IMC

See Internet Mail Consortium

IMR

See Internet Monthly Report

INTERNATIONAL CONNECTIONS ON THE INTERNET

Much of the activity on the Internet is based in the U.S. and Canada, but other countries participate as well. Some industrialized countries have tens of thousands of Internet sites, while others have few because of differences in telecommunications policies. Because of the rapidly growing popularity of the Internet in the U.S., it is likely that countries that are major trading partners with the U.S. will also get more involved with the Internet.

Europe is particularly active on the Internet. Some major organizations have helped this growth, such as EUnet, which mostly supports research sites; EARN (European Academic Research Network), which mostly supports colleges and universities; and RARE (Reseaux Associés pour la Recherche Europeènne), which is the network of networks. Japan has been more active recently with its WIDE (Widely Integrated Distributed Environment) net, although there are still relatively few people with individual Internet connections.

Finding a supplier for Internet in some countries is almost impossible. Some countries restrict Internet to only universities. Like the U.S. ten years ago, people in these countries are finding different ways to get accounts. In other countries, getting an Internet account is as easy as it is in the U.S. Of course, this will probably change over the next few years, and it will be much easier to get access in more countries.

 **FOR MORE INFORMATION**

Service:	WWW
URL:	`http://www.celestin.com/pocia/` `foreign/index.html`
Description:	A very complete guide to Internet service providers outside the U.S. This site also has a great U.S.-based list as well.

INTERNET ARCHITECTURE BOARD

The Internet Architecture Board (better known as the *IAB*) is the master body for technical changes to the Internet. Because the technology used to link together the Internet is fairly stable, any changes are usually fought in the Internet community. The IAB oversees the Internet Engineering Task Force (*IETF*) and Internet Research Task Force (*IRTF*) and ratifies any major changes to the Internet that come from the IETF. The IAB meets four times a year.

 **FOR MORE INFORMATION**

Service:	WWW
URL:	`http://www.iab.org/iab/`

Description: An overview of the work of the IAB, its members, and other information on the organization.

INTERNET ENGINEERING TASK FORCE

The Internet Engineering Task Force (*IETF*) develops and maintains the Internet's communication protocols. Although this may sound a bit dry, it is a subject that is of great concern to many Internet sites, and many people volunteer to be on the various committees. The decisions made by the IETF can have very wide-ranging effects, and must be ratified by the Internet Architecture Board before they are implemented.

Other goals of the IETF include the following:

- Identifying and proposing solutions to pressing operational and technical problems on the Internet

- Specifying the development or use of protocols to solve those problems

- Making recommendations to the Internet Architecture Board (IAB) regarding standardization of protocols and protocol usage in the Internet

- Facilitating technology transfer from the Internet Research Task Force (IRTF) to the wider Internet community

- Providing a forum for the exchange of technical information within the Internet community between vendors, users, researchers, agency contractors, and network managers

The IETF has different venues for the status reports of its various committees. Some are published in Requests for Comments documents, others as minutes of their meetings. For the technically inclined, the face-to-face IETF meetings (which happen three times a year in various parts of the world) can be incredibly interesting.

 **FOR MORE INFORMATION**

Service:	**WWW**
URL:	`http://www.ietf.cnri.reston.va.us`
Description:	This server contains sections with descriptions and status of all the IETF working groups, as well as a section with all the Requests for Comments documents.

👁 **See Also**   *Request for Comments*

INTERNET EXPLORER

Although NCSA and Netscape were the two first big players in the Web browser market, Microsoft is certainly planning on having a significant stake in it. In 1995, Microsoft released the Internet Explorer, a Web browser that works with Windows 95. Later that year, Microsoft decided to give the software away for free as a way to get Windows 95 users more in touch with the Web. Figure 2.13 shows the Internet Explorer window.

Internet Explorer is very tightly integrated with Windows 95, which lets users combine it with other Windows 95 programs easily. For example, other programs can launch Internet Explorer when the user selects a URL in the other programs' documents. Further, Internet Explorer can cause other Windows 95 programs to be launched when particular Web documents are accessed.

Figure 2.13: Internet Explorer for Windows 95

The current version of Internet Explorer does not have as many features as Netscape, but Microsoft is working to change that. Given Microsoft's huge size, and the size of the installed base of Windows 95 users, it is likely that Internet Explorer will become one of the most popular Web browsers in the coming years.

FOR MORE INFORMATION

Service: **WWW**

URL: `http://www.microsoft.com/windows/`

Description: This page leads to all of Microsoft's information about Windows 95, including Internet Explorer and related applications.

INTERNET MAIL CONSORTIUM

The Internet is much more than just the Web. In fact, there are many more e-mail users on the Internet than there are Web users. The Internet Mail Consortium (IMC) is the industry group who coordinates the future direction of e-mail on the Internet and helps promote e-mail use.

The IMC does not create any e-mail standards; instead, it helps support the Internet Engineering Task Force, who have created Internet mail standards for over a decade. The IMC also helps by getting industry consensus on what topics are important to research and standardize.

 **FOR MORE INFORMATION**

Service:	**Mail**
Address:	`info@imc.org`
Message:	help
Description:	The IMC has a complete mail server which includes information about the many Internet mail standards, FAQ documents about e-mail, and so on.

Service:	**WWW**
URL:	`http://www.imc.org/`
Description:	The same information as is available from the IMC's mail server.

INTERNET MONTHLY REPORT

So much goes on behind the scenes in the groups that help form the Internet that it is difficult for any single person to keep up. The Internet Monthly Report is a single document that is a fairly good summary of all the different groups. The purpose of these reports is to communicate the accomplishments, milestones, or problems discovered by the participating organizations.

Even beginners might find looking through a recent report interesting. By seeing what is being studied by the various task forces, you get a feel for the technical and social underpinnings of the Internet. Unless you are an Internet stalwart, it is unlikely that you will want to subscribe to the reports.

FOR MORE INFORMATION

Service:	**Anonymous ftp**
Host:	`ftp.isi.edu`
Location:	/in-notes/imr
Description:	A compendium of the monthly reports. Before copying any of these reports to your local host, be sure to check the size—some are quite large.

INTERNET RELAY CHAT

The Internet supports interactive discussions just like the phone system does. The most popular system is Internet Relay Chat, more commonly called *IRC*. IRC is, in fact, better than the common telephone conference call for getting many people in a single discussion, because dozens of people can get into a discussion without making arrangements ahead of time. IRC is used both for serious discussions and for entertainment.

IRC uses the client/server model to support communications. You run IRC client software on your computer to view and participate in the conversations; there are many clients for Unix, PCs, and Macintoshes. You then connect to one of the many IRC servers. On most systems on the Internet, simply giving the **irc** command will start a client and connect you to the closest server. On character-based Unix systems, the ircII program is by far the most popular client.

Once you are on a server, you select a *channel*, which is a name of a discussion. Some channel names have specific meanings. For example, "#Twilight_Zone" is the channel that many IRC regulars hang out in when they are not busy; it is a good place to ask beginner's questions (after reading the documentation, of course).

You control your IRC client with commands. The commands all start with a / character. The most common commands are the ones below:

Command	Description
/list	Lists all the current channels, the number of users, and the topic.
/names	Shows the nicknames of people using each channel
/who *channel*	Shows who is on a given channel, including nickname, user name and host, and real name.
/join *channel*	Joins the named channel
/nick *nickname*	Changes your nickname
/msg *nickname message*	Sends a private message to one person.

Command	Description
/help	Displays help. You can specify which command you want help on.
/whois *nickname*	Shows the "true" identity associated with a nickname.
/quit	Leaves the program

After you have joined a channel, everything you type (other than commands) appears on the channel.

Although IRC is often used for amusement, it has also been used for serious international discussions. Instead of having to set up a conference call (which often cannot allow new people to come on in the middle of the call), people will agree through mail to join a specific IRC channel at a particular time. Although the IRC medium makes discussions in which one person needs to type many long sentences difficult, many people find it more productive than telephone conferences.

FOR MORE INFORMATION

Service:	**Usenet News**
Group:	`alt.irc`
Description:	A great place to chat about various places on IRC. The FAQ for this group is particularly well-written.

INTERNET RESEARCH TASK FORCE

The Internet Engineering Task Force (*IETF*) looks at the technical issues currently affecting the Internet; the Internet Research Task

Force (*IRTF*) looks at the issues that will become important in five or ten years. As such, the IRTF gets much less publicity than the IETF, but it still has an important role in the growth of the Internet.

Some of the issues that the IRTF studies include the following:

- How will the Internet handle a billion or more individual users?

- If most of the users on the Internet come through routers, how will that affect performance and availability?

- How will having 100 million U.S. homes wired for interactive cable television affect the current users of Internet?

INTERNET SERVICE PROVIDER

In order to get access to the Internet, you need to connect to a system that is already on the Internet. For many people, this is one of the major online services such as CompuServe or America Online; for others, it is a local Internet company. All of these companies are called Internet Service Providers, or ISPs, because they provide you with Internet service, similar to the way the local telephone company provides you with phone service.

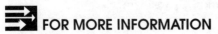 **FOR MORE INFORMATION**

Service:	**WWW**
URL:	`http://www.celestin.com/pocia/`
Description:	This is a great way to find out which Internet Service Providers offer service in your area. Although this isn't an official listing, most ISPs of any size are listed here.

INTERNET SOCIETY

The Internet Society (also called *ISOC*) has many roles. On the technical side, it is the parent society to the IETF and appoints the members of the IAB. On the users side, it supports research into how people use the Internet, helps organize educational resources for the Internet, holds the main annual Internet conference (called *INET*), and publishes a quarterly magazine. The members of the Internet Society often volunteer to help on committees and task forces that relate to their individual interests.

These are the official goals of the Internet Society:

- To facilitate and support the technical evolution of the Internet as a research and education infrastructure and to stimulate involvement of the academic, scientific, and engineering communities, (among others) in the evolution of the Internet.

- To educate the academic and scientific communities and the public concerning the technology, use, and application of the Internet.

- To promote scientific and educational applications of Internet technology for the benefit of educational institutions at all grade levels, for industry, and for the public at large.

- To provide a forum for exploration of new Internet applications and to foster collaboration among organizations in their operation and use of the Internet.

Unlike other societies in the computer field, the Internet Society doesn't control anything. It exists to keep its members informed about the Internet. It is not cheap to join ($70 per year at the time this book was published), and the only tangible benefit is a quarterly journal that covers all the aspects of the Internet Society, particularly its efforts to help bring the Internet to other parts of the world. Most members join because they want to support the goals of the Internet Society, not for the benefits they receive.

➡ FOR MORE INFORMATION

Service:	**WWW**
URL:	`http://www.isoc.org/`
Description:	This site is a good place to find out about the ISOC and other public service groups that support the Internet.

INTERNET STUDIO

Microsoft is a major player in many aspects of the Internet, particularly the World Wide Web. As the Web has grown, it has become more important for people to be able to create good-looking Web sites. Microsoft's site-creation package, Internet Studio, is a set of software tools that let you combine text, pictures, sound, and so on into a cohesive site. In this way, Internet Studio is to Internet users, what the first desktop publishing packages were to printers.

INTERNIC

The Internet grew quite large without having a central repository of information that was staffed by people; instead, it simply had a bunch of informational text files that were updated haphazardly. In 1993, the National Science Foundation awarded a five-year grant to three companies to serve as a central repository of information for Internet users and to help educate the public about the Internet. The service is called the InterNIC (with NIC being the common abbreviation for Network Information Center).

Unfortunately, the contract fell apart within a few years, and the companies are doing less than originally expected. While the most visible part of the original InterNIC was a central place where users could ask questions, that part was completely scrapped. As of this writing, the InterNIC does little other than act as a database server, and provide registration for many domain names.

FOR MORE INFORMATION

Service:	**WWW**
URL:	`http://www.internic.net/`
Description:	This is the best way to find out what the InterNIC is still doing.

See Also   *Domain Name System*

IP ADDRESSES

Every computer on the Internet has an address that can be viewed in two ways. The *domain name* is the text version of the name, such as `english.small.edu`. The *IP address* is a computer address that the computers on the Internet can deal with directly. An IP address has four digits separated by periods, such as `196.201.90.0`.

It is unlikely that you will ever need to know the IP address of a computer. In fact, because the IP for a given computer can change, you can end up using the wrong address for a computer if you use the IP address.

See Also   *Addresses, Computer; Domain Name System; ncftp*

IRC

See Internet Relay Chat

IRTF

See Internet Research Task Force

ISDN

See bandwidth

ISOC

See Internet Society

ISP

See Internet Service Provider

JAVA

The Web has inspired the creation of many new technologies. In order to deliver these to Web users, programmers wanted a way to run programs directly on Web users' computers. Sun Microsystems, a company best known for their powerful computers, invented a language system, called Java, that has become a popular method for delivering programs to users that can then be run on the users' machines.

Java has some features that make it more suitable for running from the Web than other languages. Java is specially designed to make it more secure, so you can be assured that a program you have downloaded cannot read files from your computer without your permission. Further, Java programs cannot access sensitive parts of your computer's memory.

Writing programs in Java is not easy. In fact, even if you know a more common programming language like Visual Basic or C, you may have some difficulty learning the intricacies of Java. Fortunately, you don't need to know anything about Java programming in order to run Java programs.

 **FOR MORE INFORMATION**

Service:	**WWW**
URL:	`http://www.javasoft.com/`
Description:	This is Sun's central location for information about Java, including pointers to other Web sites that relate to Java programming.

JOE

Beginning users often want an easy-to-use replacement for the **vi** editor, which comes standard with Unix. The **joe** editor has garnered a strong following on the Internet. It is full-screen, has many commands available for advanced users, but is still simple to use for text editing. Its command set is similar to the PC classic editor WordStar. **joe**'s manual is also very good. Figure 2.14 shows **joe**'s basic editing window.

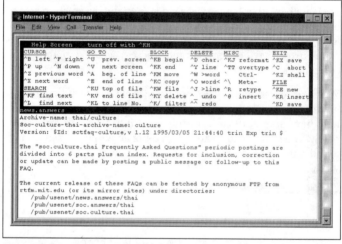

Figure 2.14: Editing with **joe**

The **joe** screen is fairly Spartan. When you start **joe**, you are in insert mode, meaning anything you type will go into the file. You can start **joe** using a file name as an argument to edit that file directly. Most of **joe**'s commands are given using the Ctrl key. Table 2.9 shows the common commands that you will use in **joe** (there are many others for advanced users). To get help at any time, press Ctrl-KH.

Table 2.9: Basic **joe** commands

Key	Action
←, Ctrl-B	Left
→, Ctrl-F	Right
↑, Ctrl-P	Up
↓, Ctrl-N	Down
Ctrl-Z	Previous word
Ctrl-X	Next word
Ctrl-A	Beginning of line
Ctrl-E	End of line
Ctrl-U	Up one screen
Ctrl-V	Down one screen
Ctrl-KU	Top of file
Ctrl-KV	Bottom of file
Ctrl-KL	Specific line
Ctrl-D	Delete current character
Ctrl-Y	Delete current line
Ctrl-W	Delete word forward
Ctrl-O	Delete word back
Ctrl-J	Delete to end of line
Ctrl-_	Undo delete
Ctrl-^	Redo delete
Ctrl-KF	Find text
Ctrl-L	Find again
Ctrl-KB	Mark beginning of block
Ctrl-KK	Mark end of block
Ctrl-KM	Move block
Ctrl-KC	Copy block
Ctrl-KY	Delete block

Table 2.9: Basic **joe** commands (continued)

Key	Action
Ctrl-KW	Write block to new file
Ctrl-KJ	Reformat paragraph
Ctrl-KO	Split window into two
Ctrl-KD	Save the current file
Ctrl-KR	Read a file into this one
Ctrl-KE	Edit a different file
Ctrl-KX	Save file and quit
Ctrl-C	Quit without saving
Ctrl-KH	Get help

Among **joe**'s best features are the block commands. You mark a block by putting the cursor at the beginning, pressing Ctrl-KB, moving the cursor to the end, and pressing Ctrl-KK. **joe** then highlights the text in the block. You can use other **joe** commands to move that block to another place, write out just that block to another file, delete the block, and so on.

Another useful feature is the one that allows you to enter file names using just the first few letters. You can type in just the first few letters and press the Tab key; **joe** fills in the rest of the name. If there is more than one file that matches that name, **joe** shows you the possible names, and you can use the ← and → keys to choose from the list. This is especially useful for long Unix file names.

joe also has features for advanced users, including the ability to search for regular expressions, window control, macro recording and playing, program editing features, the capacity to search for special characters, and so on. Be sure to read the joe manual for more information on these features.

K-12

See Education Resources

KERMIT

See File Transfers

KORN SHELL

See Shell

LIBRARY CATALOGS

College libraries were some of the earliest institutions to adopt database technology. Initially, access to the computerized library catalogs was only available by terminals in the libraries themselves; later, the catalogs were made available through the campus networks. Now, hundreds of colleges make their catalogs available to anyone over the Internet. Many non-college libraries also allow access to their catalogs.

The biggest drawback to the current system is that there are over 20 different types of software for accessing catalogs. Each has its own user interface, and the interface on some of the biggest catalogs is terribly unfriendly. In order to use a library's catalog, you have to learn a new querying system that may be of no value to you on other systems. Still, having access to hundreds of catalogs is an advantage for researchers.

Most of the college library catalogs are accessed through telnet, although some have added Gopher and WAIS access in the past few years. The popular Hytelnet program, available on most university computers, acts as a directory of all the library catalog sites. Since many libraries are just now making their catalogs available, it is important to use the latest version of Hytelnet in order to have the latest list of catalogs.

 **See Also** *Hytelnet, telnet*

LISTSERV

One of early mailing list programs that was widely used is LISTSERV. LISTSERV is most popular on computers on the BITNET network because many of those computers are IBM mainframes, and LISTSERV generally only runs on IBM mainframes. Most Internet users interact with LISTSERV programs by sending mail to them.

Most people only use LISTSERV to subscribe and unsubscribe from mailing lists. However, LISTSERV can do much more than that. It can search through old messages for specific information, it can send out updates of standard files to those who want them, and it can give you information about who else is subscribed to a particular mailing list.

How to Use LISTSERV

LISTSERV runs on many computers. When you find the name of a LISTSERV mailing list you want to be on, send mail to LISTSERV at the named host site. LISTSERV ignores the subject of the message: it only reads the mail itself. Enter the necessary LISTSERV commands in the message. Your message can have more than one LISTSERV command in it, as long as each command appears on a separate line.

For example, to join the mailing list on organic chemistry, you would send mail to `LISTSERV@RPICICGE.BITNET`. The mail can have any subject, and the contents of the message would be a single line:

```
SUBSCRIBE ORGCHE-L your-name
```

where *your-name* is your real name (not your mail address).

When it gets a message, LISTSERV processes the commands and sends back a response. For instance, when you join a mailing list, LISTSERV sends back an acknowledgment and any introductory information about the mailing list.

How to Get Information from LISTSERV

The commands for getting information from LISTSERV are listed below:

Command	Description
HELP or ?	Returns a list of commands
INFO *topic*	Returns information about that topic. The topics are

REFCARD	Command reference card
FAQ	Frequently Asked Questions
PRESENT	Presentation of LISTSERV for new users
GENINTRO	General information about Revised LISTSERV
KEYWORDS	Description of list header keywords
AFD	Description of Automatic File Distribution
FILES	Description of the file-server functions
LPUNCH	Description of the LISTSERV-Punch file format
JOB	Description of the Command Jobs feature

DISTRIBUTE	Description of Relayed File Distribution
COORDINAT	Information about LISTSERV Coordination
FILEOWNER	Information guide for file owners
DATABASE	Description of the database functions
UDD	User Directory Database User's Guide
UDDADMIN	UDD Administrator's Guide

QUERY FILE *filename filetype*	Tells the date and time of last update of the file
QUERY FLAGS	Returns technical information about LISTSERV
RELEASE	Tells who maintains the LISTSERV server and the version of the software and network data files
SHOW *function*	Returns data about the LISTSERV. The most useful functions are STATS (for general information) and NETWORK (for information about the network)

How to Subscribe Using LISTSERV

The commands for subscribing to mailing lists and checking on your subscriptions are listed below:

Command	Description
SUBSCRIBE *listname* *your-name*	Start your subscription to the named list, or change your name if you are already subscribed.
SIGNOFF *listname*	Remove yourself from the list. You can use an asterisk (*) instead of a list name to remove yourself from all lists on that server, or enter * **(NETWIDE** to remove yourself from all LISTSERV mailing lists.

Command	Description
CONFIRM *listname*	Confirms that you want to continue being on the list. You only use this command when you get a message requesting it.
SET *listname* *options*	Changes the options of your subscription. The options are as follows:

ACK or NOACK	Specifies whether or not you get acknowledgments when you post a message to the list.
CONCEAL or NOCONCEAL	Specifies whether or not to hide your name from the REVIEW command.
DIGEST	Specifies that you only want a digest of the messages, not the individual messages. A digest is the individual messages grouped together, such as ten at a time or once a day.
FILES or NOFILES	Specifies whether or not you want files (as compared to regular mail) on this mailing list
INDEX	Specifies that you only want a index of the messages, not the individual messages. An index is just the subject matter and length of the messages, no content. You can later retrieve the messages using the database functions.
MAIL or NOMAIL	Specifies whether or not you want mail (as compared to files) on this mailing list
REPRO or NOREPRO	Specifies whether or not you want to get a copy of your own messages back.
TOPICS *option*	You can specify ALL to get all topics or type + or − with a topic name to get or not get messages on a particular topic.

FULLHDR	Add full mail headers to each message you receive
IETFHDR	Add Internet-style headers to each message you receive
SHORTHDR	Add short headers to each message you receive
DUALHDR	Add dual headers (useful with PC or Macintosh mail programs) to each message you receive

How to View Mailing Lists

The commands for looking at mailing lists on a LISTSERV server are listed below:

Command	Description
QUERY *listname*	Get information on your subscription options for a list. You can specify * for the list name to see options for all the lists you are subscribed to on that server.
INDEX *listname*	Returns a directory of archive files for the list if postings are archived
STATS *listname*	Returns statistics about the list
REVIEW *listname*	Sends a list of members of the list, including the list header. You can add options preceded by a left parenthesis, such as (BY NAME. These are the options:

BY COUNTRY	Sort by country of origin
BY NAME	Sort by last name
BY NODEID	Sort by nodeid
BY USERID	Sort by mail address
NOHEADER	Don't send list header
SHORT	Don't list the subscribers

LISTS *options*   Sends information about LISTSERV
                       mailing lists. If no option is given, it sends
                       an abbreviated list of the lists at this site.
                       Other options are

DETAILED   Information about local lists with full
                  information

GLOBAL   All known lists with an abbreviated
                  description (although this still results
                  in a very long file)

GLOBAL /*xxx*   All known lists that contain *xxx* in
                  the name

SUMMARY   The membership summary for all
                  lists at this site

SUMMARY   The membership summary for all
site   lists at the named site

SUMMARY   The membership summary for all
ALL   lists at all sites (a very long file)

SUMMARY   A summary of the totals for each site
TOTAL

How to Access the File Server

The commands for files from a LISTSERV server can be used whether
or not you are subscribed to the list. The basic command to get a file is
GET *filename filetype filelist.* This command orders the specified file
or package. The filelist (similar to a disk name) is optional.

Some servers also support automatic file distribution, or *AFD*. Using AFD, you can automatically get all files that are added to the
server sent to you. You can also get just update information, called
FUI, for the files on the server. If you are interested in this service,
send mail to LISTSERV with the command **INFO AFD** to get a
document on using AFD.

How to Access Databases

Many LISTSERV sites have databases consisting of the archives of
the lists at that site. The archives are kept as databases that can be

searched using database commands. The commands for making a
database search are come from old database technology and are
slightly confusing. To get a long document on using the database
commands, use the command **INFO DATABASE**.

 **See Also**   *BITNET, Mailing Lists*

LISTS OF LISTS

A list of lists is a resource for finding information on the Internet.
The reference section in most libraries usually has a list of lists, prepared by the librarians to help researchers.

There are dozens of lists of lists on the Internet (in fact, this section is a
small list of lists of lists). Many are text files, while others are in Gopher
and World Wide Web format. Another good source of lists of lists are
the FAQs (frequently asked questions files) in Usenet news groups.
Here are a couple of popular lists of lists to get you started.

 **FOR MORE INFORMATION**

Service:	**WWW**
URL:	`http://www.uwm.edu/Mirror/` `inet.services.html`
Description:	This is the home of Yanoff's List, one of the best-known lists of lists, which is organized loosely by subject. It covers things such as health, astronomy, and games.

Service:	**Mail**
Address:	`info@justice.eliot.me.us`

Subject: *Any subject*

Message: *Any message*

Description: This is a good list of lists of legal resources on
                  the Internet, including law library catalogs,
                  anonymous **ftp** sites, and mailing lists.

Service: **Anonymous ftp**

Host: `rtfm.mit.edu`

Location: /pub/usenet-by-
                  hierarchy/sci/econ/research/econ-
                  resources-faq

Description: This is an excellent example of a FAQ that
                  is primarily a list of lists. It gives all of the
                  Usenet news groups, mailing lists,
                  anonymous **ftp** archives, and so on, that
                  are of interest to all kinds of economists.

 **See Also**   *Frequently Asked Questions*

LOGIN

On a multi-user computer, your account name is often called your
login or *login id*. The term *login* has many meanings:

- It can mean your account name.

- It is the command used on Unix computers to log in.

- It is the prompt you see on many computers when you
  first connect to them.

- It is a verb meaning to connect to a computer.

LYCOS

Lycos, based at Carnegie Mellon University, was one of the first large Web robots. It is still considered by many people to be the best starting places when you are searching for information on the Web. Figure 2.15 show's Lycos' main page.

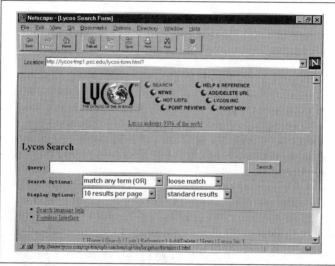

Figure 2.15: Searching the Web with Lycos

One great feature of Lycos is that it rates how popular Web sites are by counting how many times other Web sites link to them. Thus, if a particular site is listed on many other Web sites, it indicates that people making Web sites think that it's a good place to visit. This is quite different than other services, which simply tell you what the people there think is interesting.

 **FOR MORE INFORMATION**

Service:	**WWW**
URL:	`http://lycos.cs.cmu.edu/`
Description:	This is Lycos' home, and a good place to start your wanderings around the Web.

 **See Also** *robot*

LYNX

One of the better character-based interfaces for the World Wide Web is **lynx**. It uses full-screen capabilities (as compared to **WWW**, which is line-oriented), and it lets you easily move back and forth through hypertext links. **lynx** was developed at the University of Kansas for their own campus, then was released to the Internet community.

lynx is fairly easy to use. To start it, give the command with no arguments. You see the screen shown in Figure 2.16. Links are listed in boldfaced text; the link that is in reverse highlighting is the currently-selected link. All other text is unlinked information. Links can be to a wide variety of information, although **lynx** can only display text.

All **lynx** commands are single keystrokes. They are listed in Table 2.10. As you can see, there are not many, and this makes **lynx** easier to handle for most users. If you are familiar with **gopher**, you will see a lot of similarity in the commands.

To move around from link to link on a page, use the ↑ and ↓ keys. If there are multiple pages for the current file, use the PgDn and PgUp keys to move from page to page. When you find a link you want to follow (that is, to see what it is linked to), press the → key or ↵.

You can go back to the previous link by pressing the ← key. (Think of → as *go forward* and ← as *go back*.) To go all the way back to the first page you saw when you ran **lynx**, type **m**. To quit **lynx** and return to Unix, type **q**.

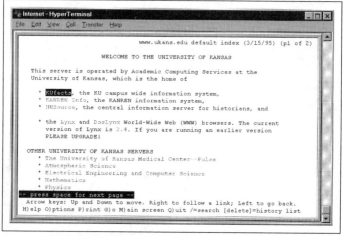

Figure 2.16: lynx initial screen

Table 2.10: lynx commands

Key	Action
↑, 8	Previous link
↓, 2	Next link
PgDn, +, Spacebar	Next page
PgUp, −, b	Previous page
→, 6, ↵	Follow current link
←, 4	Go back to previous link
m	Return to first page
q, Ctrl-D	Quit
?	Help
Backspace	List of links between first page and here
=	Show information
o	Set options
a	Add a bookmark

Table 2.10: lynx commands (continued)

Key	Action
v	View your bookmarks
p	Save in local file, mail, or print
s, /	Search pages for text
n	Search again
g	Go to a named URL link
c	Send a message to the link owner
i	Go to index
\	Switch HTML display
Ctrl-W	Refresh the screen
Ctrl-R	Reload the current page
!	Unix shell

If you have hopped from link to link for a while, you may want to see the path from your current position to the home page. Use the Backspace key to see that list. Each step on the way is remembered, and you can use the ↑ and ↓ keys to choose any step to go there directly.

At any time, you might want to see the technical information about the current document or the selected link. Type = to display a page such as the one shown in Figure 2.17. Note that the top part of the screen shows information about the current page; the bottom half shows information about the selected link.

Type **o** to set **lynx**'s options. For example, you need to tell **lynx** the name of the file you want to use on your local host to store your bookmarks. You can also specify which editor to use, your name (to appear on letters you send), and so on.

Bookmarks are links that you want to return to. To add a link to your bookmark file, simply type **a** when that link is selected (before you have taken the link). To view all your bookmarks, type **v**. You can later edit the bookmark file with any text editor.

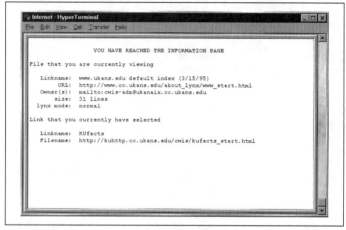

Figure 2.17: Technical information about the link

Type **p** to save the current information. You are prompted to specify where you want to save the information: to a text file on your local host, to mail to someone, or to a local printer.

Some pages have lots of links. If you know what you are looking for, type **s** to search for text. If you want to repeat the previous search, type **n**.

Typing **g** key lets you enter directly into the URL (*Uniform Resource Locator*) that you want to go to. A URL might look like `http://cui_www.unige.ch/w3catalog`, which leads to a catalog of World Wide Web resources.

Typing **c** lets you send mail to the resource owner; this is useful if you want to comment on the document. Typing **i** takes you to the main World Wide Web index in Switzerland. Typing \ changes the **lynx** display between links and the underlying HTML code that makes the links; you may find this useful if you are creating your own HTML files.

 **See Also** *HTML, Netscape, World Wide Web*

MACINTOSH ARCHIVES

The most definitive archive for Macintosh software and Mac-related files is Info-Mac at Stanford. The huge collection is well-maintained and well-organized. Unfortunately, access to the system is restricted during the daytime, and it can even be difficult to get files from there at night and on the weekends. A second site, Washington University in St. Louis, has a mirror (a duplicate) of Info-Mac and many other non-Macintosh sites with 250 incoming lines available. If you are in the Midwest or the East Coast, you should connect to Washington University instead of Stanford. There are other mirror sites outside the U.S. as well.

Of course, there are other sites that have smaller Macintosh archives. See the reference below for a complete list of those who have fewer files or more specialized collections.

Apple supports an extensive anonymous **ftp** server that has hundreds of megabytes of files. These include source code examples and lots of programming tools for developers, the latest software for Macintoshes, information on how to become a certified developer, and so on.

 **FOR MORE INFORMATION**

Service:	**Anonymous ftp**
Host:	`sumex-aim.stanford.edu`
Location:	/info-mac
Description:	The definitive collection of shareware, freeware, and text files relating to the Macintosh.

Service:	**Anonymous ftp**
Host:	`wuarchive.wustl.edu`

Location:	/mirrors/info-mac
Description:	The same information as Stanford. This site also has an incredible collection of files for PCs and Unix systems, and lots of Internet-related text files.

Service:	**Anonymous ftp**
Host:	`sumex-aim.stanford.edu`
Location:	/info-mac/info/comm/mac-ftp-list*.txt
Description:	This file lists over 100 anonymous **ftp** sites that have Macintosh files. It gives comments on many of them, telling the depth and freshness of their collections. It is indispensable for the Mac connoisseur as well as for those outside the U.S. who want to find good local access to Macintosh files. The file name might be slightly different for newer versions of the list.

Service:	**Anonymous ftp**
Host:	`ftp.apple.com`
Location:	The entire computer
Description:	Thousands of files of interest to people developing hardware and software for Apple platforms, particularly the Macintosh. There are also many programming examples, press releases, and other tidbits scattered around this site.

MACINTOSH CONNECTIONS TO THE INTERNET

There are many ways to connect a Macintosh to the Internet, depending on the type of hardware and software you have. The most common ways are the following:

- Through a modem using a standard terminal emulation program such as MicroPhone or Zterm

- Through a modem using UUCP software

- Through a modem using TCP/IP software and a SLIP or PPP connection

- Through a direct network connection such as AppleTalk or Ethernet using TCP/IP software

Each solution has its advantages and disadvantages.

Connecting with Terminal Emulation

Most Macintosh users connect to the Internet through a modem using a terminal emulation program that mimics a VT-100 terminal. With this kind of connection, the host computer does not know or care that your personal computer is a Macintosh. Everything that happens on the screen is character-based.

This is not to say that all Macintosh terminal emulation programs are the same. Some features that affect the way you interact with the Internet include the kinds of file transfer protocols (such as ZMODEM and Kermit) available, the ability to capture large text files to disk, and the ability to copy and paste text from the screen to other Macintosh programs.

Connecting with UUCP

Connecting to the Internet using Unix's UUCP protocol is probably the least common method for Internet service. Using UUCP, you can only send and receive mail and Usenet news, and those are both done in batches, not interactively. For example, when you want to send mail from your Macintosh to the Internet, you create the messages, then run the UUCP connection software; that software sends your outgoing mail, gets your incoming mail, and disconnects. You cannot run other Unix software, such as a Gopher client or anonymous **ftp,** on the host.

Using UUCP does have some advantages. If the telephone call to your closest Internet host is expensive, you want to make the most of each call, and UUCP does that well. If most of what you want from the Internet is news and mail, a UUCP connection might be sufficient.

There are a few shareware and commercial Macintosh programs that support UUCP connections. There are both mailing programs and Usenet news readers that know how to send and receive as UUCP clients; some software can handle both mail and Usenet news.

How to Connect through SLIP or PPP

The previous two methods describe how to be a user on an Internet host. However, you can become an Internet host yourself by connecting your Macintosh to a host computer through the TCP/IP protocol on which the Internet is built. This normally is more expensive than simple terminal emulation, but it is very useful if you want to be connected for long periods of time and want an interface that is more Mac-like.

In order to connect as a TCP/IP host over a modem, you have to run one of two protocols: SLIP or PPP. Both of these protocols allow two computers connected through a serial line (such as a modem) to interact using TCP/IP. The two protocols have the same results, but SLIP seems to be much more popular than PPP, although PPP is considered to be technically better.

Being a host on the Internet has many advantages. You can transfer files to your Macintosh using **ftp** instead of having to download them using a ZMODEM or another protocol. You can also make files from your Macintosh available to others on the Internet. If appearances are important to you, your system gets to have its own domain name instead of you being a user on someone else's system.

To run SLIP or PPP, you need to run the standard networking software on your Macintosh, then add the TCP/IP software on top of that, and SLIP or PPP on top of that. There are many sources for the TCP/IP software and the SLIP or PPP software. You also need to have a host that is willing to let you connect as a SLIP or PPP client. The process of setting up the software is pretty technical and is best left to someone with networking experience.

Connecting through a Network

The second method for connecting to the Internet through TCP/IP is by far the better one: get a direct connection through a network. There are two major advantages of this method over SLIP and PPP: speed and reliability. Even the slowest network is faster than the fastest common modem in use today. Thus, file transfers are faster both for you and for people whom you want to access your system.

SLIP and PPP are inherently less reliable than a direct connection because they rely on clean phone lines. Even with error-correcting modems, a bad phone connection can cause TCP/IP to have to re-send information many times. Some programs that work fine with a direct connection barely work with SLIP or PPP connections, even though they should appear the same (but slower) to applications.

TCP/IP-Based Macintosh Software

Another big advantage of using TCP/IP through a modem or through a network is that you can also use software that has a very Mac-like interface. There is very good freeware, shareware, and commercial TCP/IP software available for the Macintosh.

 **FOR MORE INFORMATION**

Reference:	**Anonymous ftp**
Host:	`sumex-aim.stanford.edu`
Location:	/info-mac
Description:	Almost every freeware or shareware Macintosh program for Internet connection is available from this server. In addition, there are many helpful text files describing how to make various kinds of connections to the Internet.

MAGAZINES, ON-LINE

Just as there are many books that are available on-line, there are also many magazines that are available for free on the Internet. In fact, many magazines are published only on the Internet and are not distributed on paper. You can subscribe to almost all on-line magazines and receive them through the Internet mail system. The back issues of most magazines are also available by anonymous **ftp**.

Unfortunately, there is no central repository of on-line magazines, and it is almost impossible to get a comprehensive list of all the on-line magazines that exist. Most people just stumble into the ones they want by reading about them in Usenet news groups that relate to the magazine or on mailing lists.

See Also   *Books, On-Line; Project Gutenberg*

MAIL

One of the mainstays of the Internet has always been mail (sometimes known as electronic mail or email). The ability to send a letter to anywhere in the world with almost no effort has helped fuel the Internet's explosive growth. The mail system used on the Internet is showing its age, but it has held up well so far.

Like other services on the Internet, mail is a client-server system. Your host computer acts as the server for your mail, receiving it from other Internet sites and storing it for you. You run a client program to handle your mail (to read it, save it, send new mail, etc.). It is important to remember that the mail system is not unified: you can use many different kinds of clients for a particular kind of mail server.

Mail is passed between computers on the Internet using a protocol called SMTP, or Simple Mail Transfer Protocol, which is part of TCP/IP. On each system, other programs convert the messages that come through SMTP into messages for its users. When your mail client asks for your mail, other programs make it available. These programs are not part of SMTP, but are specific to the operating system and software run at your site. No one other than system administrators and network gurus need to know much about SMTP, because it is so far removed from the users.

Some mail clients are not particularly smart. Unfortunately, one of the most-used clients, the Unix **mail** program, is one of these. It has a clunky user interface and does not give you much information while you are using it. Other mail clients are smarter. Two common Unix mail clients, **elm** and Pine, have much nicer interfaces and give you many more features than **mail**. The **emacs** editor also has a very complete mail client in it. Because of the importance of mail to many Internet users, other mail clients with even more intelligence have been created. They all use the same server, but present you with very different views and capabilities.

If you are on a large network, you probably have many choices. For example, there are many powerful mail clients that run under the XWindows system. Seeing mail as part of a graphical interface often helps you prioritize and scan for important messages. In the past few years, a new protocol called POP (Post Office Protocol) has come into existence.

For example, Figure 2.18 shows the Microsoft Exchange mail client that comes with Windows 95.

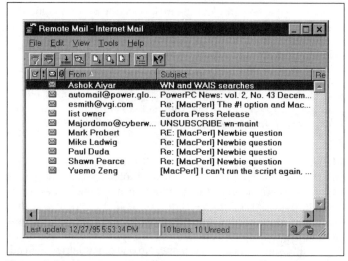

Figure 2.18: Reading mail with the Windows 95 Exchange mail client

How to Look at Mail Messages

Every mail message on the Internet comes with certain information attached. Some of that information is quite valuable; other is of little interest. Each mail message consists of two parts: the header and the content. The header is all of the information such as who sent the message, when it was sent, and to whom it was sent. The content is what was typed in the body of the message.

Most mail clients show you only a small part of the header:

```
Return-Path: <finaid@ihtfp.edu>
To: chrisr@english.small.edu
Cc: jgoal@ihtfp.edu
```

```
Subject: Re: Several Questions
Date: Mon, 15 Feb 1994 20:01:52 +1100
Sender: finaid@ihtfp.edu
```

The return path and the sender are not always the same, particularly for mail from mailing lists. (The full header often contains much more information, such as information about each stop the mail took between the sender and the receiver; this is rarely interesting.)

The Cc: line lists the carbon copies that were sent to others. Each person receiving the mail sees the names in the To: line and the Cc: line. There is another option: blind carbon copies. Blind carbon copies are those sent to others without their names being listed in the headers. Note that some versions of **mail** do not process these correctly and the people in the blind carbon copy list are shown in the message header. Thus, using blind carbon copies should probably be avoided (you can instead duplicate the message and send it separately).

There can be many other lines in a header. For example, some mailers support the concept of *precedence*, which allows bulk mail to be passed along at a lower priority than regular mail. Also, newer mail-sending systems have additional lines, such as the type of content, the character set used, and even the name of the program used to mail the letter.

As mentioned before, you may want to use a different mail client instead of **mail** if it is available to you. However, many systems only allow you to use **mail**, and you will probably find this sufficient.

How to Use Unix's mail Program to Send Mail

Sending mail with **mail** is quite easy. Simply give as the argument to the **mail** command the address of the person to whom you want to send mail:

```
% mail sandy@rgb.ivideo.com
```

mail then prompts you for the subject; enter any text you want to appear in the Subject line of the received message. You may also see a Cc: prompt. Enter the names of anyone you want to get a copy of this message or simply press ↵ to go on.

After the subject and Cc: lines, you get no more prompts. Type in the message you want to send. When you are finished with the message, press Ctrl-D to with the cursor positioned on a line by itself. This finishes the letter and causes **mail** to send it, then returns you to the Unix prompt. If you realize as you are typing the letter that you do not want to send it, press Ctrl-C twice to abort the mail.

Because the **mail** program doesn't let you edit what you enter except with the Backspace key, you cannot change anything on a line that has already been entered. It is much better to use an editor to create a text file that looks exactly the way you want it to and then send the contents of the text file.

As you type, there are many commands you can give. You must give these commands only at the beginning of a line, not in the middle. Table 2.11 lists the commands you can give while composing mail (these commands are sometimes called *tilde escapes* because each starts with the tilde character, ~).

Table 2.11: **mail** sending commands

Command	Description
~e	Start the editor that you have specified in Unix's EDITOR variable. This is clearly preferable to typing without an editor.
~v	Start the editor that you have specified in Unix's VISUAL variable. This is clearly preferable to typing without an editor.
~r *filename*	Read the file into the message.
~w *filename*	Write the message text (not the header) into the given file.
~.	Stops message input (same as Ctrl-D).
~q	Quit from entering the letter, saving any input to the file dead.letter. Unlike Ctrl-D or ~., this does not send the letter.
~x	Same as the ~q command but does not save the message in the dead.letter file.
~?	Get help with mail sending commands.

Table 2.11: mail sending commands (continued)

Command	Description
~h	Prompt for the four major header lines: Subject:, To:, Cc:, and Bcc:. If you have already filled in those header lines, you can edit them using the Backspace key.
~t *names*	Add names to the To: line.
~s *subject*	Change the subject line.
~c *names*	Add more carbon copy (Cc:) names to the message.
~b *names*	Add more blind carbon copy (Bcc:) names to the message.
~d	Read in the file called dead.letter. This is usually where letters that could not be delivered are stored, so you can use this command when you resend the letter.
~<! *shell-command*	Read input from Unix's standard output.
~!, ~! *command*	Run the Unix shell. You can also give a shell command as an argument to run just that one command.

The ~r command is one of the most useful. Assume that you are typing a letter to someone and want to include the text from a file called *results* in the letter. You would enter something like this:

```
Here are the data that we got yesterday.
~rresults
"results" 36/1213
Let me know what you think.
```

The line after the ~r command is displayed by **mail**. It shows the number of lines and characters in the file you read in.

How to Use Unix's mail Program to Read Mail

When you give the mail command, it displays a brief list of what you have in your mailbox. Figure 2.19 shows an example of the list you might see.

```
Internet - HyperTerminal
File  Edit  View  Call  Transfer  Help

proper.com:/user/chrisr# mail
Mail version 5.5 6/1/90.  Type ? for help.
"/var/mail/chrisr": 10 messages 9 unread
>U  1 mike@twinpeaks.prc.c  Wed Dec 27 10:29   77/3266  "Re: [MacPerl] Newbie "
 U  2 esmith@vgi.com         Wed Dec 27 11:51   63/2634  "Re: [MacPerl] The #1 "
 U  3 paul.duda@qm.sprintc   Wed Dec 27 12:55   58/2406  "Re: [MacPerl] Newbie "
 U  4 zeng0007@gold.tc.umn   Wed Dec 27 14:04   36/1545  "[MacPerl] I can't run"
 U  5 spearce@injersey.com   Wed Dec 27 15:41  131/5771  "Re: [MacPerl] Newbie "
 U  6 mark_probert@yes.opt   Wed Dec 27 16:01   65/2622  "RE: [MacPerl] Newbie "
    7 eudora-dude@listserv   Wed Dec 27 15:50  109/5995  "Eudora Press Release"
 U  8 automail@power.globa   Wed Dec 27 14:23  184/8443  "PowerPC News: vol. 2,"
 U  9 Majordomo@cyberwerks   Wed Dec 27 14:25   17/721   "UNSUBSCRIBE wn-maint"
 U 10 aiyar@biochemistry.B   Wed Dec 27 16:06   39/1571  "WN and WAIS searches"
&
```

Figure 2.19: List of messages shown by **mail**

The & is **mail**'s prompt for commands. There are many possible commands; the most common are shown in Table 2.12.

Many **mail** commands take an optional argument, *message*, which refers to a "message list." This tells **mail** what message you want to act on. If you don't specify which message, **mail** performs the command on the current message. You can specify:

- a message number (such as 2)

- a range of messages (such as 2–5)

- all messages (using *)

- all messages from a particular user (using the user's name)

- all messages on a particular subject (using / and the word in the subject)

Table 2.12: mail receiving commands

Command	Description
p *message*	Display the messages using Unix's **more** command. To display the currently-selected message, you can simply press ↵ instead of a command.
n	Select and display the next message
cd *directory*	Change to the directory, or to your home directory if you do not specify one
d *message*	Delete the messages
dp *message*	The same as the d command followed by the p command
u *message*	Undelete the messages
r *message*	Reply to the sender of the messages
R *message*	Reply to the sender and all recipients of the messages
e *message*	Start the editor that you have specified in Unix's EDITOR variable
v *message*	Start the editor that you have specified in Unix's VISUAL variable
s *message file*	Append the messages to the named file
w *message file*	Append the messages to the named file without headers
S *message*	Appends the messages to a file that has the same name as the return address of the first message. For example, if the message is from finaid@ihtfp.edu, this would be appended to the file named finaid.
m *names*	Send mail
=	Display the current message number
h	Display full message headers
pre *message*	Hold the specified messages in the system mailbox instead of the mbox file

Table 2.12: mail receiving commands (continued)

Command	Description
x	Quit without changing the system mailbox
q	Quit and move all messages that were not deleted to the mbox file
top *message*	Show only the top lines of messages
file *mailbox-file*	Stops reading the current mailbox and starts reading mail from the named file. This is useful for reading from the mbox file.
!	Unix shell escape
?	Display help

For example, to delete messages 2, 3, 4, and 5, you would give this command:

```
& d 2-5
```

The **s** and **w** commands are very handy for saving messages that are sent to you. If you use consistent file naming conventions, you can save all of the messages from a certain person or concerning a certain topic in a particular file.

How to Use Other mail Options

You saw above how you can start **mail** with some options (such as the -s to name a subject or < and a file name to send a file). There are many other useful options you can use to start **mail** with:

Option	Description
-e	Checks to see whether you have mail. If you don't, you are simply returned to the Unix prompt.
-f *mail-file*	Reads your mail from the named file instead of the system mailbox

Option	Description
-H	Displays the list of headers for your mail but doesn't let you read them
-N	Starts **mail** without showing you the list of messages

Note that the way **mail** acts when you start it may be different at different Unix sites. When **mail** starts, it looks in two files: /usr/lib/Mail.rc and .mailrc on your home directory. Those files can contain mail commands that change the way that **mail** behaves. You can change the contents of the .mailrc file yourself; for example, you can change the storage location of files that you save.

 **See Also** *Addresses, Mail, elm, File Transfers, Mailing Lists, Pine, SMTP*

MAILING LISTS

Before Usenet news groups became popular, the most widespread method of distributing information to groups of people was mailing lists. Mailing lists are still very popular today for many reasons:

- Many people find them easier to use than Usenet news groups

- Some Internet sites, particularly BITNET sites, do not have access to Usenet

- Some groups want to restrict who can read or post to them

There are two types of mailing lists. Most mailing lists simply send a copy of each message that is sent to the central mail address to everyone on the list. Other mailing lists run special software that collects many messages into a single message before passing it on; these combined messages are often called *digests*. Some lists let you choose whether you want each message or just the digest.

There are thousands of mailing lists, and they cover almost every subject. Some have only a few members, others have thousands. Before you sign up for mailing lists, you should remember that you may receive dozens or hundreds of new mail messages a day, and you may have a hard time keeping up with all the mail. On the other hand, mailing lists are an excellent way of keeping track of the latest developments in diverse fields.

Mailing List Rules

Although each list is different, there are a few general rules to adhere to when subscribing to a mailing list (others are described in the "Etiquette" entry). The first and foremost rule is to remember that what you post to the list can be read by thousands of people with diverse backgrounds. Don't assume that everyone is interested in everything that you say or will understand the way that you say it. Keep in mind that not everyone will share your opinions. Think before you post.

Another rule has more to do with the mechanics of mailing lists. Most lists have a separate address from the main address for requests asking to get on and off the list. Never send subscription or removal requests to the list itself if there is a different address for those requests. Such requests break down the continuity of discussions on the mailing lists and are annoying.

Another good rule is to send responses to questions posted on the list directly to the person who posted the question, not to the whole list. For example, if someone asks whether anyone has experience with a particular piece of hardware, 50 people might respond, and others on the list wouldn't want to see 50 responses of "I do."

On the other hand, if you've received interesting information through private mail from a question you asked in mailing list, be sure to summarize the answers and post them for the whole group to see. This prevents the same questions from coming up repeatedly.

How to Find Mailing Lists

Because there are so many mailing lists, you need a list of lists to know what is available. Unfortunately, there are many lists of lists. The information in them overlaps, and they are all very large.

If you just want to browse one of the lists of lists to see what is available, pick any of the ones listed below. Check with your system administrator to see whether or not one of the lists is kept on your system, so that you don't waste disk space and system resources downloading it. If you are looking for a narrow topic, your best bet is to use WAIS to search the mailing-list database to look for the particular topic.

How to Start a Mailing List

There are many kinds of host software that help create and maintain mailing lists. The most popular is LISTSERV, which is the mainstay of the BITNET network. Other systems that run on Unix hosts and have many management features are also available; two popular ones are Listserver and Majordomo. Some sites prefer not to run mailing list managers because of the increased mail traffic that they often bring. Talk to your system administrator to find out whether or not you can start a mailing list based at your site.

 **FOR MORE INFORMATION**

Service:	**WWW**
URL:	`http://www.neosoft.com/internet/paml/`
Description:	This list contains the most active mailing lists and is updated often. You can also get the latest version of this list from the Usenet news news.answers group.

Service:	**Mail**
Address:	`listserv@bitnic.educom.edu`

Subject: *Any subject*

Message: LIST GLOBAL/*text*

Description: This will return a list of all the LISTSERV mailing lists that relate to that text (assuming the text appears in their descriptions). Note that if you just put **LIST GLOBAL** in the message, you will get a list of all LISTSERV mailing lists back, and this file is incredibly long.

◉ See Also *LISTSERV, Mail*

MCIMAIL

MCIMail was one of the first commercial electronic mail services. It was never very successful because of its unfriendly user interface and high prices. However, some companies adopted it as their basic in-house mail package (particularly if they adopted MCI's long-distance services early on), and it still exists today. You can send mail to an MCIMail user either at her or his user number or login name, followed by @mcimail.com.

MICROMUSE

See MUD

MILNET

The MILNET is the non-classified portion of the U.S. Defense Department's network. MILNET is connected to the Internet, and many MILNET sites are active participants in the Internet culture, with individuals at those sites posting to Usenet news groups and mailing lists regularly. The MILNET is also a testbed for U.S. security research on Internet security.

MIME

Regular mail can only contain ASCII characters because of the limitations of SMTP, the protocol used to pass mail between Internet computers. In the past few years, this limitation has become a major problem as more people want to pass pictures, sound, and formatted text. To address these problems, a new standard called MIME (which stands for Multipurpose Internet Mail Extensions) was developed. MIME allows arbitrary data to be included in mail messages, as long as the header in the mail message identifies the content so that the mail client can read it.

In order to use a message with MIME content, you need a mail client that has MIME capabilities. The Unix mail program, **mail**, doesn't have these capabilities, but most other modern mail programs do. Note that some mail readers support more MIME capabilities than others. For example, **elm** and Pine are character-based programs, so they don't support displaying pictures or playing sounds; however, they do support reading messages that use the MIME standard for breaking a message into separately-readable parts.

MIME has other features that will help establish it as the standard protocol to use in the future. For example, you can add formatting (such as **bold** and *italics*) to your plain text messages; you can break a single message into many parts so that the reader can skip parts he or she is not interested in; you can send video segments; and you can even define your own type of data (such as a new kind of picture file) for inclusion.

As more people create MIME-enhanced messages, there will be more demand for MIME-compliant mail readers. Within a few years, it will be normal to get voice- and video-mail over the Internet as easily as text mail.

FOR MORE INFORMATION

Service:	**Anonymous ftp**
Host:	`rtfm.mit.edu`
Location:	/pub/usenet-by-group/comp.mail.mime/mime-faq
Description:	This document describes what MIME is, the kinds of things that MIME is good for, where to find out more about MIME, and how to find software that supports MIME.

MIRROR

Many anonymous FTP sites on the Internet are very busy, sometimes so busy that people who want to use them can't get on. As a service to the Internet community, other sites have a copy of all the files on the busy site so that people can choose from many places to get their files. These duplicate sites are called *mirrors* because they are an exact reflection of the original site. Many mirror sites update their files every night, bringing them up to date with their source sites almost immediately.

Using a mirror instead of the main site can often be better for another reason: it might be closer to you, and thus the time it takes to transmit a file is shorter. For example, there are mirrors in Europe,

Asia, and Australia of popular U.S. FTP sites. Users on those continents can get their files far more quickly and efficiently from local mirrors than from the source sites.

MISC.

See Usenet News

MOO

See MUD

MOSAIC

The Mosaic family of programs were the first popular Web browsers. Some Mosaic programs are free, while others are part of commercial packages. They can handle many formats of information, such as pictures and sound. There are versions of Mosaic for Unix running XWindows, Windows for the PC, and Macintosh.

You can get some forms of Mosaic off the Internet, while others can be bought with other software or with books. For example, you can get CompuServe Mosaic, with the book *Mosaic Access to the Internet* by Daniel A. Tauber and Brenda Kienan (Sybex, 1995). This book also has in-depth instructions on using the software and on creating your own home page.

Figure 2.20 shows a typical screen from Mosaic for Windows 95. You can see that the visual presentation of the information is very

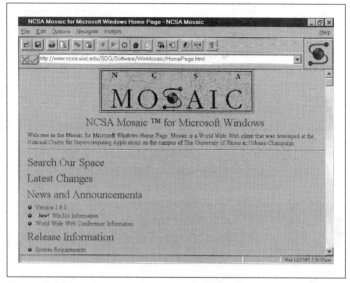

Figure 2.20: Browsing the Web with Mosaic

different from that of lynx, for example. Mosaic displays graphics, headings in different type and point sizes than other text on the screen, and highlighting for the links. Mosaic is very configurable, so you can specify what fonts and colors to use for the various kinds of information in the hypertext documents.

Mosaic programs were originally written and distributed by NCSA, the National Center for Supercomputing Applications. NCSA was founded in 1985 by the National Science Foundation in order to distribute expensive supercomputer resources to universities and research centers. As part of its mission, NCSA has created many free programs to make connecting to the Internet easier. The Mosaic programs are some of the best examples of high-quality, free Internet resources.

Although Mosaic is a very popular graphical program for looking through the World Wide Web, it is not the only one that you can get. Two other such programs are Netscape from Netscape Communications and Internet Explorer from Microsoft.

FOR MORE INFORMATION

Service:	**WWW**
URL:	`http://www.ncsa.uiuc.edu/SDG/` `Software/SDGSoftDir.html`
Description:	This site contains copies of the latest versions of Mosaic for all supported systems.

See Also *HTML, Netscape, World Wide Web, WWW*

MUD

A MUD (which stands for Multiple User Dimension or Multiple User Dungeon) is an interactive, multiplayer environment that is similar to the dungeon games that became popular in the late 1970s. A MUD is somewhat like Internet Relay Chat, but with lots of gaming rules thrown in. In a MUD, you become a character in a story and interact with other people who are playing the game at the same time. You play in a MUD using the **telnet** program to connect to a host that is running a MUD program.

MUDs can be fairly elaborate, with lots of rules and many players at different times of the day. The person programming the MUD (sometimes referred to as "God") can allow or disallow a wide variety of interactions between players and the environment.

 FOR MORE INFORMATION

Service:	**Usenet News**
Group:	rec.games.mud

Description: This group, and the groups below it in the
                    hierarchy, discuss MUDs and MUD
                    players. You can find a list of the hundreds
                    of MUD sites around the world on the
                    rec.games.mud.announce group.

 **See Also**   *Games*

NATIONAL INFORMATION INFRASTRUCTURE

The National Information Infrastructure, also known as the *NII*, is the
name that the U.S. government attached to the Internet and other public networks. The government wants to move the NII forward as a
way of giving the U.S. an advantage in education, worldwide trade,
international commerce, and health care. Though the language of the
proposal is still vague, it is clear that there will be a large investment by
Congress in supporting the NII in the coming decade. It is also clear
that there will be a large clash over who runs which parts of the infrastructure: the government or private companies.

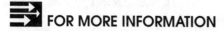 **FOR MORE INFORMATION**

Service: **Anonymous ftp**

Host: `ftp.ntia.doc.gov`

Location: /pub/agenda.deb.txt

Description: This file describes the current status of the
                NII as well as the government's goals in
                promoting it. It also describes the various
                task forces within the administration that
                are working on specific parts of the NII.

NATIONAL RESEARCH AND EDUCATION NETWORK

The major federal initiative to give better access to networked information to all students is called the National Research and Education Network, or NREN. The bill, which was signed into law and is now in the study and implementation phase, would help bring tens of thousands of schools onto the Internet. The NREN faces many hurdles before it becomes a reality, including the fact that many K-12 schools don't have enough modern computers (if any) to make the access useful. The NREN may fund new computers for some schools, but to what extent that will happen is not yet clear.

Another problem in implementing the NREN is the extent to which it will be controlled by the government. Many telecommunications companies provide better Internet access to business and residence customers, and they may want to provide NREN access as well (for a price, of course).

 See Also   *Consortium for School Networking, Education Resources*

NCFTP

Getting files from anonymous **ftp** servers is one of the most useful functions of the Internet. Unfortunately, the ftp program is not very friendly. Its user interface is something that only a Unix guru could love. **ncftp** is a program that was developed to make transferring files by ftp easier.

ncftp has a similar user interface to ftp, but it gives you more information, makes better guesses about what you want, and gives you

more options. If you already know how to use ftp, you can use
ncftp without learning any new commands, because **ncftp** understands all of ftp's commands. It expands greatly on ftp's advanced
features as well.

ncftp has many convenient commands:

- It assumes that you want to give the user name **anonymous** and the password of your mail address when you
  open a host system. This saves you from typing (or mis-
  typing) those each time you open a host. You can override
  this easily.

- If you put the names of the sites you often use in a preferences file, you don't have to type the full name. For example, you can abbreviate *rtfm.mit.edu* as just *mit*.

- **ncftp** remembers the name of the directory you visited the
  last time you opened a particular site. **ncftp** immediately
  takes you to the last directory you visited when you open
  a site.

- You can have **ncftp** repeatedly try to access sites that
  are busy.

- You can specify the path and file name of the file you
  want on the command line and have it downloaded automatically. This makes getting files completely automatic.

- You can set options in your preferences file, such as the
  name of the Unix program you want to use as your pager.
  You can also change these options while running the
  program.

- The **ncftp** prompt can be changed to give you much
  more information. Instead of showing ncftp>, you can
  have the prompt tell you the name of the directory you
  are looking at.

- You can view a text file on the remote machine through a
  paging program such as **more** instead of having to view
  the whole thing at once or downloading it and reading it
  locally. You can also view a directory listing through the
  paging program.

- You can use wildcard characters when you use the **get** command to match a single file name.

- You can convert domain names to IP addresses and vice versa through an incredibly handy feature.

- You can keep a log of your interactions with **ncftp**.

Even with all these changes, using **ncftp** is quite similar to using ftp. Read the section on "ftp" in addition to reading this one since only the differences are listed here.

Opening Hosts When Starting ncftp

ncftp automatically logs you in as **anonymous** and gives your mailing address as the password when you open a host. This prevents you from having to type it each time and speeds the process of logging on. You can override this by preceding the host name with **-u**:

```
% ncftp -u chem.small.edu
Login Name (chrisr):
Password:
User chrisr logged in.
```

In this case, the user pressed ⏎ at the Login Name prompt, then entered her password. This logged her in as herself, not as anonymous.

As with regular **ftp**, you can keep a file called .netrc that lists the names of the sites you commonly log into. This file can also contain other **ncftp** commands, as you will see later. If you have a .netrc file, you don't have to type the full name of the host you want to open, just enough characters for **ncftp** to recognize it.

e.g. EXAMPLE

Assume that your .netrc file looked like this:

```
machine rtfm.mit.edu
machine mac.archive.umich.edu
```

```
machine wuarchive.wustl.edu
machine ftp.apple.com
machine sumex-aim.stanford.edu
```

You could open the sumex-aim.stanford.edu site with one of these commands:

```
% ncftp sum
```

or

```
% ncftp aim
```

This is because sum and aim don't appear in any of the other machine names in the file. Likewise, you could save lots of typing by opening wuarchive.wustl.edu this way:

```
% ncftp wu
```

How to Open Hosts within ncftp

ncftp makes opening sites that you have already been to even easier. If you give the **open** command with no host name, you are shown the last 20 sites you opened, as well as all the sites in your .netrc file. You can then pick the desired site by typing its number. For instance, assume you want to open some site that you opened recently, but all you remember is that it had "bio" in the name:

```
ncftp> open
Recently called sites:
  1. BLOOM-PICAYUNE.MIT.EDU
  2. bloom-picayune.mit.edu
  3. ftp.halcyon.com
  4. enh.nist.gov
  5. zaphod.ncsa.uiuc.edu
  6. cica.cica.indiana.edu
  7. biochemistry.bioc.cwru.edu
  8. caisr2.caisr.cwru.edu
. . .

(site to open) #7
```

Some sites, particularly those with freeware and shareware for personal computers, get so busy that they reject people trying to log in. You will often receive a message such as *Too busy now, try later*. If you are trying to get to one of those sites, using the **-r** option will cause **ncftp** to keep retrying the connection until it is successful.

You can also use the **-r** option before the site name on the command line.

How to Get Files Automatically

Often, you use **ncftp** to get a single file that you already know the name of, such as a file named in this book. You can create a single command to do this from the Unix command line. Follow the host name with a colon and the path of the file; **ncftp** understands this as a request to log on, change to the directory, get the file, and log off. For instance, to get the file /pub/listing from the host ftp.small.edu, you would use this command:

```
% ncftp ftp.small.edu:/pub/listing
%
```

You can also use this technique from within **ncftp**:

```
ncftp> open ftp.small.edu:/pub/listing
ncftp>
```

You do not have to specify a file when you are using this technique. If the item you specify is in fact a directory instead of a file, **ncftp** simply opens the host and changes to that directory for you.

How to Set ncftp Options

Set **ncftp**'s options with the **set** command. The most common options are listed in Table 2.13. Use the **show** command to show the current settings.

Give the option commands at the command line.

```
ncftp> set progress-reports 4
```

Table 2.13: ncftp options

Option	Description
anon-open	Tells whether to automatically use anonymous as the login name
anon-pass-word	The password to use when anonymously logging in
local-dir	The directory into which files will be saved
logfile	The name of the file to log your ncftp sessions. Leave this blank to prevent logging
logsize	How many lines to include in the log file
mprompt	Tells whether or not to prompt for each file when using the **mget** command
netrc	Name of the startup file
prompt	The prompt string to display
progress-reports	The kind of progress reports you want to see as a file is being transferred. 0 prevents progress reports during file transfers. 1 shows the percentage, 2 displays a bar graph, 3 shows just the number of kilobytes transferred, and 4 displays a dot for each 10% transferred.
recent-list	Specifies whether or not to remember the recent sites you've opened
tips	Specifies whether or not to display the opening tip on how to use ncftp
type	The type of transfer in use (ascii or binary)

You can also put **set** commands in your .netrc file, preceded by a #
(so that **ftp** thinks that they are comments). For example, the top of
your .netrc file might look like this:

```
#set progress-reports 4
#set verbose 2
#set prompt "@C> "
```

The last line above shows how to use special character combinations in your prompt string to show useful information about your session. These are the additional combinations:

String	Meaning
@D	Full path name on remote computer
@J	Current directory name on remote computer
@H	Name of remote host
@C	Name of remote host and full path name, separated by a colon
@c	Same as @C except followed by a newline character
@E	Number of commands you have given
@M	Displays *(Mail)* if you receive mail while running **ncftp**
@B	Make the following text bold
@I	Make the following text italic
@U	Make the following text underlined
@R	Make the following text reverse
@P	Make the following text plain text
@N	A newline character

You could use the following to show you what host and directory you are in:

```
set prompt "@C> "
```

This would change the prompt to something like this:

```
ftp.cso.uiuc.edu:/doc/pcnet>
```

How to View and Retrieve Files

It is easy to read text files on remote systems while using **ncftp**. The **page** command lets you see the contents of a file one page at a time. (The **page** command runs the Unix **more** command within **ncftp**.)

This is very useful if there is an index for a directory and you want to see what the files are before downloading them. For instance, to see a file called *index*, you would give this command:

```
ncftp> page index
```

To see long directory listings a page at a time, use the **pls** and **pdir** commands. These commands correspond to ftp's **ls** and **dir** commands, except that the output stops at each screen.

Retrieving files is also easier with **ncftp**. You do not need to type the full name of the file in order to get it. If you can use wildcards to select just one file, the **get** command will retrieve it. This is particularly useful for long or complicated file names, like the ones used on FAQs.

How to Use Advanced Features

The **lookup** command lets you convert domain names to IP addresses and vice versa:

```
ncftp>lookup 204.1.1.23
ivideo.com
 204.1.1.23
ncftp>lookup ivideo.com
ivideo.com
 204.1.1.23
```

As you use **ncftp**, you may want to keep a log of the commands you give as a way to document your searches. To do this, use the **set** command to give a file name for the log and the number of lines that you want to appear in the log:

```
ncftp>logfile "ncftp.log"
ncftp>logsize 5000
```

You can also put these commands in your .netrc file.

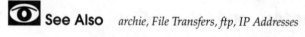 **See Also**   *archie, File Transfers, ftp, IP Addresses*

NCSA

People who have been on the Web for a few years know NCSA as the home of Mosaic, the first popular graphical Web browser. NCSA is also the creator of the most popular Web server, called NCSA httpd.

NCSA, which stands for the National Center for Supercomputing Applications, created Mosaic as a way to help scientists interact with each other better. Of course, the Web is now much more than just a network for scientists. NCSA is based in Champaign, Illinois, and is a spin-off from the University of Illinois at Urbana-Champaign.

 **FOR MORE INFORMATION**

Service: **WWW**

URL: `http://www.ncsa.uiuc.edu/`

Description: NCSA does much more than create Web applications. This site has lots of information about NCSA's other computer-related projects.

 **See Also** *Mosaic*

NETFIND

The Netfind program can look in many databases to help locate a user on the Internet. Because there are so few databases of users, searching with Netfind is often unsuccessful.

To use Netfind, use the **telnet** command to connect to one of the following host sites:

- `bruno.cs.colorado.edu`

- `ds.internic.net`

- `mudhoney.micro.umn.edu`

- `netfind.oc.com`

- `redmont.cis.uab.edu`

Log in with the name **netfind**. The prompts you see will be different depending on the site. Generally, you are prompted for the person's name and any identifying information that you can give, such as the domain of her or his host.

 **FOR MORE INFORMATION**

Service:	**Mailing List**
Name:	Netfind
Address:	`netfind-users-request@cs.colorado.edu`
Subject:	*Any subject*
Message:	*Any request to join the mailing list*
Description:	This list mostly describes the Netfind software, although there is sometimes discussion of Netfind's limitations.

See Also   *Addresses, Mail*

NETIQUETTE

See Etiquette

NETSCAPE

For a while, many people thought that Mosaic would be the only popular Web browser. In the end of 1994, however, Netscape Communications released its Netscape Navigator browser, and it was an instant success. The browser, most commonly called just "Netscape", is now by far the most popular Web browser, and many people credit it with helping fuel the rapid growth of the Web.

Netscape has many features that are unique, and Netscape Communications is putting more in all the time. In early 1996, Netscape version 2 was released, giving users even more features in a single package. For example, Netscape version 2 can be used not only as a Web browser, but as a mail client as well.

Netscape's Various Views

Many Netscape users only use Netscape as a traditional Web browser. Figure 2.21 shows Netscape viewing a typical Web page that has both graphics and text. Netscape can also play sounds from within the browser if you go to a page with sound files.

Netscape also has a Usenet news reader, shown in Figure 2.22. The news reader window has three panels. The upper left panel lists all of the Usenet news groups that you have available to you, while the upper right panel lists the messages that you have not read in a selected news group. The bottom panel shows the selected message.

Some people also use Netscape to read their mail, although most people use a dedicated mail program for this. Netscape's mail window is almost identical to its Usenet news window, as shown in Figure 2.23. In the mail window, the upper left panel shows your different mail boxes, while the upper right panel shows all the messages in the selected mailbox.

Configuring Netscape for Mail and News

Using Netscape is quite easy, once you have it set up. However, there are some important settings that you need to know about

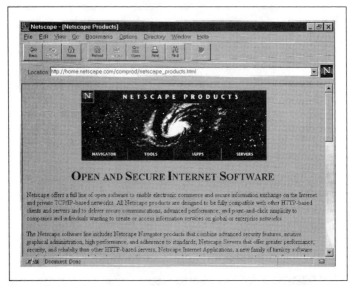

Figure 2.21: Netscape's Web viewer

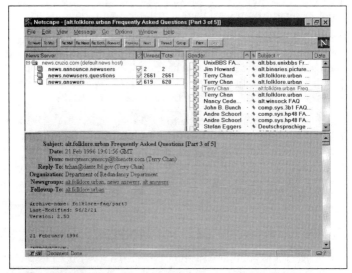

Figure 2.22: Viewing Usenet news groups with Netscape

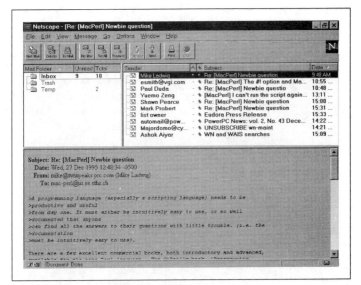

Figure 2.23: Using Netscape to read your mail

before you start clicking away. All of Netscape's main configuration is in the Options menu, in dialog boxes with tabs across the top of them. Choosing a tab brings up a different dialog box.

Netscape comes configured to work correctly for basic Web browsing. However, there are some options that you have to set before you can use Netscape to read Usenet news or your mail. These settings are part of the Mail and News Preferences dialog box, in the Servers tab, shown in Figure 2.24. In this dialog box, you must enter the domain name for your SMTP server, your POP server, and your news server; your Internet service provider will tell you what names to enter here.

Extending Netscape

Netscape is one of the few browsers that let you add features that did not come with the browser. These features, called plug-ins and modules, are created by other companies and link themselves to Netscape in a predictable fashion. Netscape provides a few plug-ins of its own, and there are dozens of other plug-ins available free on the

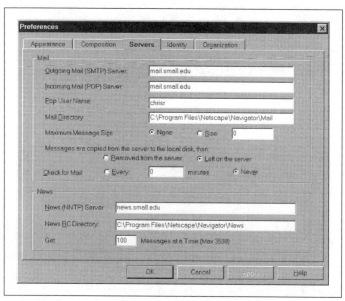

Figure 2.24: Setting mail and news hosts

Internet or from software manufacturers. You can find out which plug-ins are officially supported by visiting Netscape's home site.

 **FOR MORE INFORMATION**

Service: **WWW**

URL: `http://home.netscape.com/`

Description: This is Netscape's official server for all information about its products. This server also has links to Netscape's FTP servers where you can download trial versions of their software.

 **See Also**   *Mosaic, World Wide Web, WWW*

NETWORK FILE SYSTEM

An early problem with networks was that accessing files over a network often forced the user to use bizarre syntax in their file requests. To solve this problem, Sun Microsystems developed a protocol called Network File System (better known as *NFS*). NFS is built into operating systems, and computers using NFS can access files over a network as if the files were local. The protocol is widely used on the Internet.

NETWORK INFORMATION CENTER

The generic name for the department that helps users with network problems is the Network Information Center, or *NIC*. Many universities and large corporations have NICs, as do other organizations that rely heavily on their networks.

 **See Also**   *InterNIC*

NETWORK NEWS TRANSFER PROTOCOL

As Usenet news got more popular, standards needed to be set on how news articles would be posted. The protocol on how computers should update news with new articles from their users is called Network News Transfer Protocol, or *NNTP*.

NEWS

See Usenet News

NFS

See Network File System

NIC

See Network Information Center

NII

See National Information Infrastructure

NN

The number of messages posted to Usenet news groups increases every month. While it used to be easy to follow all of the news groups you were interested in, it is almost impossible today without help. **nn** was designed to make reading Usenet news quicker by showing you only the subject lines of the messages in a particular news group and letting you choose which ones you want to read. **nn** has a full-screen character-based interface and can run on essentially all Unix computers.

Novice and intermediate users may find **nn** to be a bit intimidating because it has so many features. However, the features for advanced users can be ignored, and the interface for basic features is pretty simple. Almost all **nn** commands are one or two letters. **nn** commands are case-sensitive, meaning that typing **a** has a different effect than typing **A**. There are more choices than in the **rn** program, but getting through a long list of news groups goes much faster in **nn**.

nn determines which news groups you want to read by looking in the file called .newsrc in your home directory. **nn** first checks to see which of the news groups listed in that file have messages that you haven't read. It then shows you a menu of the unread articles from the first group in the list. Working with this list is called *selection mode*. You select the articles that you want to see, then move into *reading mode*, looking at each of the articles in succession. When you have read all of the selected articles from the first group, **nn** switches you back to selection mode for the next group, and so on.

Having two modes makes reading busy news groups go quickly. You can see what articles are about, whether there are already responses to them, and so on, on a single screen (or on multiple screens if there are more than 19 unread articles). This is especially handy in news groups that you are only marginally interested in. For example, assume you are interested in school issues. Only a few of the articles in misc.kids are about education, and you can usually tell which ones those are from the headers. In selection mode, you choose those articles and skip the rest.

nn arranges articles by subject, with replies to an article coming after the original article. A group of replies and replies to replies is called a *thread*, because a thread of an idea runs through all of them. If you are interested in a topic, you might want to read the whole thread, particularly if the thing that starts the thread is a question (hopefully, some of the replies are answers). **nn**'s organization by thread is the main reason that many people prefer it over **rn**.

How to Prepare Your .newsrc File

If you have run a news reader such as **rn**, **nn**, or **tin** before, skip this section. It describes how to set up your .newsrc file before running either program for the first time.

One major problem with **nn** is that it makes a wrong decision the first time you run it: it assumes that you want to subscribe to all the news groups in the universe. On many systems, that is over 5000; clearly, this is a wrong assumption.

To avoid this, simply create a file named **.newsrc** in your home directory and include the names of the news groups that you know that you are interested in. You can use any text editor to create this file.

Each line in your new .newsrc file should just have the name of a news group followed by a colon. For example, your file might look like this:

```
alt.health.ayurveda:
comp.simulation:
news.announce.newgroups:
news.announce.newusers:
```

The groups can be in any order: **nn** will present them in the order in the file.

How to Start nn

nn has many command line options. Normally, you will start **nn** with no options; this tells it to look in your .newsrc file and then start looking in the named groups for new articles.

If you want to look at one or a few groups, you can list them on the command line as well:

```
% nn comp.answers rec.answers
```

The first time you run **nn**, you may want it to "catch up" with all articles. This essentially tells **nn** that you do not want to read any old articles. To do this, use the **-a0** option:

```
% nn -a0
```

If you have only some idea of the name of the group you want to enter, use the **-g** option. **nn** prompts you for the name— type **?** and **nn** will tell you all the possible groups that match. For example, if you know you want to look at a group in comp.sys.mac, you could enter the following command:

```
% nn -g
```

```
Enter Group or Folder (+./~) comp.sys.mac.?
advocacy announce app comm databases digest
  games hardware hypercard misc oop.
  portables programmer scitech system wanted
```

If you want databases, type **d** and press the Tab key to complete the name, then press ↵.

At any time in **nn**, typing **Q** will quit the program.

Selecting Which Articles to Read

Once you have selected a group (or **nn** has selected it for you from your .newsrc file), you are presented with the first selection mode screen. An example is shown in Figure 2.25. The top line tells you the name of the news group you are viewing and the number of articles. The second line from the bottom tells you that you are in selection mode and how far along you are in the group (the percentage of the articles read). The bottom line is reserved for messages from **nn**.

Notice that many of the articles do not have their own subjects. Instead, the subject is > or >> and so on. > indicates a reply to an article, while >> indicates a reply to a reply; these are the threads described above. If the original article is not shown, the first article shown may start with one or more > symbols, meaning that the oldest article is not what started the thread.

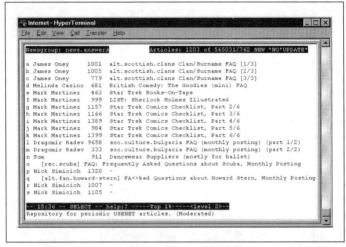

Figure 2.25: nn selection mode screen

The way the articles themselves appear on each line depends on your choice for the layout. There are five layout modes, and each shows a letter (which is how you choose the articles you want to see) and the subject of the articles. Some layout modes also show the name of the person who posted the article and/or the number of lines in the article.

To see all the layouts, type " (quotation mark) to cycle through the five choices. To find out the number of the layout you are currently using, give the **:set layout** command followed by a space; this displays the number on the bottom line. You can type in another number (from 0 to 4) to change the setting. For now, assume that you are using layout 4, shown in Figure 2.25.

There are two basic ways to select an article:

- Type its letter, such as **c**

- Use the ↑ and ↓ keys to move the selection to the desired letter and type **.** (period)

It is likely that you will want to select more than one article at a time. To select everything in the thread of a selected article, type *****.

To select a range of articles, type the letter of the first article, followed by **-**, then the letter of the last article (as in **b-e**). To the selection, select the article again.

If the news group has more than 19 articles, it will span across more than one page. Use the > and < keys to see the next or previous pages. The $ key takes you to the last page, and the ^ key takes you to the first.

How to Go from
Selection Mode to Reading Mode

You can use the Spacebar key to move forward from page to page. When you press the Spacebar key while viewing the last page, you switch into reading mode for the current news group.

You can switch into reading mode using two other commands:

- Typing **Z** goes to reading mode but then returns to the current news group when you are finished reading the selected articles.

- Typing **X** goes directly to reading mode without allowing you to select anything on pages you haven't seen yet. This is handy if there are many pages of articles that you don't want to even scan.

You can also preview articles while in selection mode (this gets a bit confusing). Type % and the letter of the article you want to preview. **nn** either shows the article on its own screen or at the bottom of the selection mode screen. You can page through the article or even preview the following articles. To quit preview mode, type **q**.

There are three additional useful selection mode commands. Typing **N** skips reading mode for a news group and takes you directly to the next news group. Typing **P** takes you back to selecting in the previous group; this is useful if, after reading articles in reading mode, you want to go back and scan more articles. Typing **Y** shows you an overview of the groups you have not read yet.

If you want to see a group that is not in your .newsrc file, give the **G** command and enter the name of the group. **nn** gives you the prompt shown below:

```
Group or Folder (+./~ %=sneN)
```

Type the name of the group. To get **nn** to help you, press Spacebar to complete an entry or type **?** to see your choices. After you specify the group, **nn** gives you this prompt:

```
Number of articles (uasne) (a)
Use: j)ump u)nread a)ll @)archive s)ubject
 n)ame e)ither or number
```

Press ↵ or type **a** to see all the articles, which is the usual choice. Type **s** and enter a subject, **n** and enter a name, or **e** and enter text to look for in either field. You can also enter a number, and **nn** will show you just that many of the entries (the most recent ones).

If you want to unsubscribe to a news group, type **U**. This removes the file from your .newsrc file. If you are not currently subscribed (for example, if you got to the group using the **G** command), the **U** command subscribes you and writes the entry in your .newsrc file.

Table 2.14 summarizes the commands for selection mode.

How to Read Articles

In reading mode, you are presented with each of the selected articles one at a time. The top of the screen tells you which article you are reading and the date it was posted. The bottom of the screen tells you the group you are reading, how many more you have selected, and how far through the article you are.

If the article is more than one page long, press the Spacebar key to go to the next article. Pressing the Backspace key goes to the previous page. The D and U keys take you half a page forward or backward. The $ key takes you to the last page, and the ^ key takes you to the first page.

In long articles, you may want to search for a particular word or phrase that you are interested in. Type /, then type in a regular expression (which is usually just search text), and press ↵. To find

Table 2.14: nn selection mode summary

Command	Description
"	Cycles the article layout between the five choices
:set layout	Shows the current layout number and allows you to specify a different number
letter	Selects the article with the label of that letter
.	Selects the article where the cursor is
*	Selects all the articles with the same subject as the current article
letter-letter	Selects all the articles in a range
>	View next page
<	View previous page
$	View last page
^	View first page
Spacebar	View next page
Z	Go to reading mode, but then return to this news group
X	Go to reading mode, skipping the rest of the pages in this news group
%letter	Preview the article with the label of that letter
N	Skip this news group, coming back to it later
P	Return to selection mode for the previous news group
Y	Overview of upcoming groups
G	Go to a specific group
U	Unsubscribe or subscribe to the current group

the same text again, you can type a . without typing in the text again.

To see a full header, type **h**. If an article is encoded with rot13 encoding (such as for risque jokes), type **D** to decode it. If the article has many tabs and spaces and is hard to read, type **c** to compress them.

As you are reading, you may want to save interesting articles to a disk. There are three similar commands to do this: s, o, and w. All three save the article; s saves it with full header, o saves it with a short header, and w saves it with no header. **nn** prompts you for the name of the file you want to save to. If you don't like the default name, press Backspace or Ctrl-W and type in a new one. You learn below how to change the default names suggested.

When you are on the last page of an article, pressing the Spacebar key goes to the next article. If you do not want to read more of the article, type n to go to the next article without finishing the current one. To go back to the previous article, type p. If you wish to deselect all selected articles about a subject, type k to skip the articles and move on.

If you want to go back and select additional articles about a subject, type *. Type a or b to select the article after or before the current one, even if you didn't select it in selection mode.

How to Post and Reply

As you are reading an article, you may want to reply to it. There are three different ways to reply:

- Type **R** to send mail to the person who posted the article

- Type **M** to send mail (possibly including the article) to someone else

- Type **F** to reply in the news group, adding your message to the thread

Your chosen editor opens. Write your message and save it as you normally do. **nn** then asks you whether you want to send the message or discard it.

An interesting feature of **nn** is that it makes it difficult to post a new article. You must give the **:post** command (there is no single key command). **nn** then prompts you for the group to post to; if it is the current group, just press ⏎. **nn** prompts you for the other information, then lets you edit your new posting.

How to Go from
Reading Mode to Selection Mode

When you are on the last article and press Spacebar or type **n**, **nn** takes you to selection mode for the next news group. Thus, the normal progression of using **nn** is select, read, select, read.

While you are in reading mode, you may want to go back to selection mode for the current group, probably to select more articles. To do this, type =. On the other hand, you may want to skip all the rest of the marked articles; type **X** to go directly to the next group. You can also type **N** to save the rest of the selected articles to read later.

Table 2.15 summarizes the commands for reading mode.

Table 2.15: **nn** reading mode summary

Command	Description
Spacebar	Go to next page
Backspace	Go to previous page
d	Display half a page forward
u	Display half a page backward
$	Show last page
^	Show first page
/	Search for text
.	Search again
h	Show full headers
D	Show with rot13 decoding
c	Compress spaces and tabs
s	Save with full headers
o	Save with short headers
w	Save with no headers
n	Go to next article
p	Go to previous article
k	Skip over articles in this thread
*	Select all articles in this thread

Table 2.15: nn reading mode summary (continued)

Command	Description
a	Read next article, whether or not it was selected
b	Read previous article, whether or not it was selected
R	Reply to the author in mail
M	Send mail to another person
F	Create a follow-up message in the thread
:post	Post a new message
=	Go back to selection mode for this news group
X	Skip the rest of the selected articles in this group and go to selection mode for the next group
N	Go to selection mode for the next group, keeping the remaining selected articles unread

How to Use Advanced nn Features

nn has many advanced features, far too many for this book to cover. Here are a few of the major ones so that you can get an idea of how configurable and flexible it is.

When you run **nn** the first time, it creates a directory called .nn in your home directory, and creates a file called "init" in that directory. When you start **nn**, it executes the commands in the init file first. The commands look like this:

```
set layout 4
set default-save-file +$G
```

The first line tells **nn** to use layout style 4 each time. The second line tells **nn** the format for the default names for the s, o, and w commands. The + signifies the default News directory in the home directory, and the $G signifies that the name be the group name, such as alt.dreams.

You can get **nn** to search through all news groups for a particular word in the subject line. This is useful when you don't know which news group might have the discussion you want. There are a few command line options that help in the searching:

Option	Description
-s*word*	Specifies a word to look for in the subject lines.
-n*word*	Specifies a name to look for in the names on articles.
-m	Merges the found articles into one group. Without this, **nn** would display them group by group.
-x	Look in unread and read articles.
-X	Look in unsubscribed and subscribed groups. Note that this can take a very long time.
all	Use this as the name of the group at the end of the command line.

For example, to search for all articles in all groups with the word *iguana* in the subject, give this command:

```
% nn -mxX -siguana all
```

If you want to know more about how to use **nn**'s advanced features, be sure to read the on-line documentation.

 **See Also** *Usenet News*

NNSC

See NSFNet

NNTP

See Network News Transfer Protocol

NREN

See National Research and Education Network

NSFNET

The NFSnet is the part of the Internet that is supported and maintained by the U.S. National Science Foundation. The NSFnet was the high-speed backbone of the Internet, although other providers also support high-speed links. This is described in detail in Part 1.

OCLC

See Online Computer Library Center

ONLINE BOOK INITIATIVE

The Online Book Initiative™, also know as OBI, is a group of people trying to collect and distribute freely available material on the Internet. By freely distributable, they mean

- anything that is not copyrighted in the original (such as U.S. government documents)

- anything that the copyright owners allow for virtually unlimited copying (with some possible restrictions, such as that no one can modify the work or sell it for a profit)

- anything whose copyright has run out

The OBI emphasizes the first two kinds of material in its efforts.

➡️ FOR MORE INFORMATION

Service:	**Anonymous ftp**
Host:	`ftp.std.com`
Location:	/obi
Description:	This directory and the ones under it contain all of the texts currently available as well as information about the OBI. The README file describes the contents and organization.

👁 **See Also**   *Books, On-line; Project Gutenberg*

ONLINE COMMERCE

One of the fastest ways to make a new technology popular is to make it handle money in a way that nothing else does. The Internet has the potential for fundamentally changing the way we deal with banks and stores. For example, you can pay many of your bills using the Web; some banks even let you view your monthly checking statement online.

Taken to its extreme, the Internet could be used as a different kind of money system. A variety of companies are making it possible to pay for purchases on the Internet without directly using credit cards; in fact, some are creating new forms of cash that can only be used on the Internet.

It is still not clear how significant all these changes will be to the average Internet user. Banks are very conservative, and are only slowly allowing novel services to be conducted online. Credit card companies are moving faster, but even they are being cautious, given the large problems with Internet security. In a few years, we will probably have a better picture of how popular the Internet is for commerce.

 See Also *CommerceNet*

ONLINE COMPUTER LIBRARY CENTER

The Online Computer Library Center, better known as OCLC, is one of the primary sources for library cataloging information in the U.S. They run an extensive fee-based database search catalog called FirstSearch that is available to libraries and individuals. It references other databases and makes searching for academic and business information easy (although it is not cheap).

 **FOR MORE INFORMATION**

Service:	**Mailing List**
Name:	FirstSearch
Address:	`listserv@oclc.org`
Subject:	*Blank*
Message:	subscribe firstsearch-l *your-name*
Description:	This list is a discussion of the FirstSearch database and the other offerings of OCLC.

ORACLE

The Oracle is an experiment in interactive on-line humor. People post questions to the Oracle, who is supposed to be an all-knowing god. However, the questions are answered by other people on the Internet. The questions and answers are moderated, and can be quite humorous. To read the questions and answers, subscribe to the Usenet news group rec.humor.oracle.

 **FOR MORE INFORMATION**

Service:	**Anonymous ftp**
Host:	`cs.indiana.edu`
Location:	/pub/oracle
Description:	This directory has all of the previous postings. The files named *help* tell you how to submit questions to the Oracle and how to become one of the answerers.

PACK

The **pack** command is similar to the **compress** command. However, the **pack** command is not used nearly as often as the **compress** program on most Unix systems. You can tell that a file has been compressed with **pack** because it has a .z at the end of its name. (Note the lowercase .z: and uppercase .Z indicate the file was compressed with **compress**.)

The **pack** program takes a single argument, the name of the file to be compressed. The result is a file with the same name but with .z at the end, such as "spiral-picture.z". It removes the original (large) file and replaces it with the compressed file.

NOTE

The original file is deleted and replaced with the compressed file. You should only use **pack** with files that you do not need to access in their uncompressed forms.

The **unpack** program can only uncompress files that were compressed with **pack**.

 **FOR MORE INFORMATION**

Service:	**Anonymous ftp**
Host:	`ftp.cso.uiuc.edu`
Location:	/doc/pcnet/compression
Description:	An excellent list of all the compression schemes in common (and not-so-common) use on PCs, Macintosh systems, Unix, IBM mainframes, and Amiga computers. It also tells where to get the freeware and shareware programs.

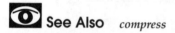 **See Also**   *compress*

PC ARCHIVES

The best source of PC software is Washington University in St. Louis. This site has mirrors of the most popular IBM PC sites. One of the primary sites for which Washington University is a mirror is SIMTEL, which used to be on a military computer but is now on a computer at Oakland University in Rochester, Michigan.

➡ FOR MORE INFORMATION

Service:	**Anonymous ftp**
Host:	`wuarchive.wustl.edu`
Location:	/systems/ibmpc
Description:	This site also has an incredible collection of files for Macintoshes, Unix systems, and lots of Internet-related text files.

Service:	**WWW**
URL:	`http://www.coast.net/SimTel/`
Description:	SimTel is the best-known collection of shareware and freeware for PCs running MS-DOS, OS/2, and all flavors of Windows. You can easily search for the kind of software you want here.

PC CONNECTIONS TO THE INTERNET

There are many ways to connect an IBM-compatible computer to the Internet, depending on the type of hardware and software you have. These are the most common ways:

- Through a modem using a standard terminal emulation program such as HyperTerminal, a program that is part of Windows 95

- Through a modem using UUCP software

- Through a modem using TCP/IP software and a SLIP or PPP connection

- Through a direct network connection such as Ethernet using TCP/IP software

Each solution has its advantages and disadvantages.

Connecting with Terminal Emulation

Most PC users connect to the Internet through a modem using a terminal emulation program that mimics a VT-100 terminal. With this kind of connection, the host computer does not know or care that your personal computer is a PC. Everything that happens on the screen is character-based.

This is not to say that all PC terminal emulation programs are the same. Some features that affect the way you interact with the Internet include the kinds of file transfer protocols (such as ZMODEM and Kermit) available, the ability to capture large text files to disk, and the ability to copy and paste text from the screen to other PC programs. Also, many people find that using Windows communications software is easier than character-based MS-DOS programs.

Both Windows 3.1 and Windows 95 come with terminal emulation programs. The program that comes with Windows 3.1, called Terminal, is very rudimentary and does not offer many features. However, HyperTerminal, which comes with Windows 95, is fairly robust and has many features of value to Internet users.

Connecting with UUCP

Connecting to the Internet using Unix's UUCP protocol is probably the least common method for Internet service. Using UUCP, you can only send and receive mail and Usenet news, and those are both done in batches, not interactively. For example, when you want to send mail from your PC to the Internet, you create the messages, then run the UUCP connection software; that software sends your outgoing mail, gets your incoming mail, and disconnects. You cannot run other Unix software (such as a Gopher client or anonymous **ftp**) on the host.

Using UUCP does have some advantages. If the telephone call to your closest Internet host is expensive, you want to make the most of each call, and UUCP does that well. If most of what you want from the Internet is news and mail, a UUCP connection might be sufficient.

There are a few shareware and commercial PC programs that support UUCP connections. There are both mailing programs and Usenet news readers that know how to send and receive as UUCP clients; some software offers both.

Connecting through SLIP or PPP

The previous two methods describe how to be a user on an Internet host. However, you can become an Internet host yourself by connecting your PC to a host computer through the TCP/IP protocol on which the Internet is built. This normally is more expensive than simple terminal emulation, but it is very useful if you want to be connected a great deal and want to have an interface that is more like the other MS-DOS or Windows software that you run.

In order to connect as a TCP/IP host over a modem, you have to run one of two protocols: SLIP or PPP. Both these protocols allow two computers connected through a serial line (such as a modem) to interact using TCP/IP. The two protocols have the same results, and SLIP seems to be much more popular than PPP, although PPP is considered to be technically better.

Being a host on the Internet has many advantages. You can transfer files to your PC using **ftp** instead of having to download them using a ZMODEM or another protocol. You can also make files from your PC available to others on the Internet. If appearances are important, your system gets to have its own domain name instead of you just being a user on someone else's system.

To run SLIP or PPP, you need to run TCP/IP software that knows how to interact with other hosts through SLIP or PPP. This software comes as part of Windows 95, but not as part of Windows 3.1 or MS-DOS. Also, there are commercial TCP/IP software packages for Windows 95 that improve on the software that Microsoft supplies with the operating system. There are many sources for TCP/IP software.

Most TCP/IP software comes with its own connection to SLIP or PPP, but in some cases you must also get separate SLIP or PPP software.

You also need to have a host that is willing to let you connect as a SLIP or PPP client. The process of setting up the software is fairly technical and is best left to someone with networking experience. If you are running a PC-based Unix operating system, it may have TCP/IP built in, making the configuration a bit easier.

 NOTE

Some SLIP and PPP software requires that you have a 16-bit UART chip controlling the serial ports on your PC. However, most PCs in use have only an 8-bit UART chip. Again, be sure to find out before downloading or purchasing the software.

Connecting through a Network

The second method for connecting to the Internet through TCP/IP is by far the better one: have a direct connection through a network. There are two major advantages of this method over SLIP and PPP: speed and reliability. Even the slowest network is faster than the fastest common modems in use today. Thus, file transfers are faster both for you and for people who you want to access your system.

SLIP and PPP are inherently less reliable than a direct connection because they rely on clean phone lines. Even with error-correcting modems, a bad phone connection can cause TCP/IP to have to re-send information many times. Some programs that work fine with a direct connection barely work with SLIP or PPP connections even though they should appear the same (but slower) to applications.

TCP/IP-Based PC Software

Another big advantage of using TCP/IP through a modem or through a network is that you can also use software that has a more PC-like interface; this is particularly true for Windows-based software. There is very good freeware, shareware, and commercial TCP/IP software available for both MS-DOS and Windows.

For example, Figure 2.26 shows a Usenet news client for Windows 95 called Free Agent. Although many Web browsers also have Usenet news clients in them, some of the external news applications like Free Agent have more features, or a better interface, than the news clients built into the browsers.

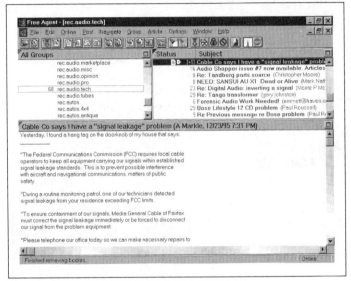

Figure 2.26: Free Agent news client for Windows 95

PEACENET

PeaceNet is a bulletin board system linking many non-profit organizations, religious organizations, and individuals concerned with peace and social justice. It was one of the first systems that helped bring together diverse local groups so that they could discuss organizing disparate groups. The discussions revolve around such areas as human rights, disarmament, and international relations.

To send mail to someone on PeaceNet, use the person's account name and give the machine name igc.apc.org. Thus, you might send mail to `chrisr@igc.apc.org`.

 **FOR MORE INFORMATION**

Service: **WWW**

URL: `http://www.peacenet.apc.org/`
`peacenet/`

Description: A great deal of information about PeaceNet, news items about peace activities around the world, and links to many other pacifist and progressive groups on the igc network and the Internet.

 **See Also** *EcoNet, igc*

PEM

See Privacy Enhanced Mail

PICO

The Pine mail reader is very popular, and many people got used to the small text editor in it. That editor, **pico**, is available separately. It has fewer features than other small text editors like **ee**, but it is more widely available. In **pico**, most of the screen is blank, with some of the available commands shown at the bottom.

As you would expect, you move around text using the ↑, ↓, ←, and → keys. Use Ctrl-A and Ctrl-E to move to the beginning and end of the line, and Ctrl-V and Ctrl-Y to move forward and backward by page. Use the Backspace key to delete before the cursor or Ctrl-D to delete after it.

pico has a limited ability to move a block of text. Press Ctrl-^ to mark one end of the text you want to move, move the cursor to the other end (you see the text being selected as you move), and press Ctrl-K to remove the block of text. Move the cursor to the position you want to move the block, and press Ctrl-U.

Searching for text is easy. Press Ctrl-W and enter the text to search for. You can also have **pico** check the spelling in a document by pressing Ctrl-T. You are prompted, in alphabetical order, for each word that is not recognized.

You can read a file into **pico** with the Ctrl-R key. To write the current file, press Ctrl-O. To quit, press Ctrl-X.

A few more commands that may be useful:

- To get help at any time, press Ctrl-G.

- To neaten the right margin of a paragraph, press Ctrl-J.

- To redisplay the current screen, press Ctrl-L.

- To see the current cursor position, press Ctrl-C.

👁 **See Also**   *Pine*

PINE

The importance of mail to Internet users is clear, and many people find the standard Unix **mail** program too difficult to use for reading mail. Pine is a popular replacement for reading and sending mail. Pine offers many features to all levels of users, and is available on many systems where **elm**, another good mail program, is not available.

Using Pine is easy, and its on-line help is quite complete. Most commands in Pine are single letters; a few are Ctrl-key combinations. Most of the commands available at any time are shown at the bottom of the screen. If there is not enough room for all the commands, typing **o** shows you another set of commands. Note that all commands are shown in uppercase letters, but you can type them as either upper- or lowercase.

When editing or reading messages, Pine uses the same commands as **pico**. In fact, **pico** is an offshoot from Pine. If you are familiar with **pico** commands, you will find using Pine simple.

Pine's initial screen is shown in Figure 2.27. To read your mail, type **i**; to create new mail, type **c**. Type **q** to quit from Pine. These are the three commands from the main screen that you will give most often.

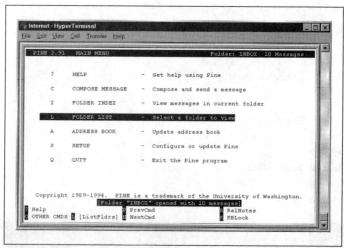

Figure 2.27: Initial Pine screen

 NOTE

Most Pine screens allow you to print with the y key. However, most Unix hosts do not support user printing. Thus, you should generally avoid using this command. This was included in Pine because there are versions of Pine that work on personal computers that are attached to a network and, of course, printing on personal computers is acceptable.

How to Use Pine's Mail Folders

Pine uses *folders* to hold mail. You can have many folders; in fact, you always start with at least three. The INBOX folder is the mail that has not been read; this is the mail delivered by the mail server on your system. To see the available folders, or to choose a new folder to read, type l in the main menu.

By default, Pine also creates two folders called *sent-mail* and *saved-messages*. The sent-mail folder keeps a copy of all the mail you send. The saved-messages folder can be used to save important messages.

To choose a folder, type **L** in Pine's initial screen. In this screen, you can choose a different folder from the default INBOX folder. For example, you can use Pine to look through all the messages that you have sent by choosing the sent-mail folder. Use the ↑, ↓, ←, and → keys to select a new folder to view. You can create new folders by typing **a** (you can also create new folders as you are reading your mail).

Note that the word *folder* may be a bit confusing. Other than the INBOX folder, folders are actually files that are kept in the directory called mail in your home directory. Think of a folder as a place where messages are stored.

How to Use Pine to Read Mail

To see the index of your incoming mail, type **i** from the main menu. This takes you to a screen that looks like Figure 2.28. Each line on the screen is a message to you.

A typical line looks like this:

```
+ A 1   Nov 21 maint@marfin.com
(756) New release available
```

The columns contain the following information:

- The status of the mail

- The message number

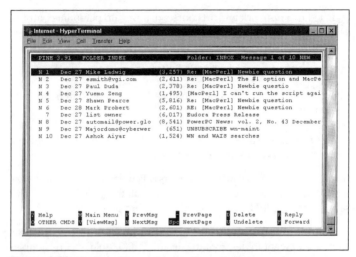

Figure 2.28: Index of incoming mail

- The date it was mailed

- Who mailed it (this often gets cut short)

- The number of characters in the message

- The subject

There are two characters in the status line of the message. The first character is + if the message was directly to you, not as part of a mailing list or on a Cc: list of the message. The other letter in the status can be:

Letter	Description
A	You have answered the message
D	Waiting to be deleted
N	New message

Use the ↑ and ↓ keys to choose a message to view. If there are too many messages to fit on the screen, use the Spacebar and - keys to move forward and backward by pages. You can also jump to a specific message number by typing **j**. After you have selected a message you want to look at, type **v** or press ↵.

When you are reading a message, most of the commands are the same as for when you are looking at the index. When you are finished reading a message, type **i** to get back to the index.

There are many actions you can take on the selected message in the index or on the message you are reading:

Command	Description
r	Reply to the sender of the message
f	Forward the message to someone else
s	Save the message to a folder
e	Save the message in a text file
d	Mark the message for deletion
u	Undelete the message if it is marked for deletion

Remember that Pine can look in one of many folders. You can change folders easily by typing **g** and choosing the desired folder. You can also sort the folder you are looking in by typing **$** and choosing the order (by subject, by sender, etc.).

How to Send Mail with Pine

To create a message, type **c** from the main menu (you can also do this from many other menus). The To:, Cc:, and Subject fields at the top of the screen are the same as in other mail programs. Note that you can enter a nickname from your address book (described later) in the To: field.

The commands you can give while editing the message are different than those you can give while entering the fields at the top of the message. The editing commands are shown at the bottom of the screen and are the same as those in **pico**. The new commands you can give while editing the fields at the top of the message are these:

Command	Description
Ctrl-R	Show full header

Command	Description
Ctrl-O	Postpone this message until later, returning to the main menu
Ctrl-X	Send the message
Ctrl-J	Add an attachment to the letter; note that this is only useful if the other person also has Pine
Ctrl-T	Add this address to the address book

How to Use the Address Book

If you often send letters to the same person or same group of people, you will find Pine's address book incredibly useful. A *nickname*, which is stored in the address book, is a shortcut for a mailing address. For instance, if you regularly mail to `sandy@rgb.ivideo.com`, you could make a nickname of *sandy*. Nicknames are also good for making a single name for a group of people to whom you send the same message.

You can make address book entries by typing **a** from the main menu. However, there is a faster way. When someone you want in your address book sends you a message, type **t** while reading the message or while the message is selected in the index. This takes you to the address book and fills in the name and address, saving you from having to type them in (and possibly making spelling mistakes).

How to Edit the Pine Configuration File

Pine creates a configuration file called .pinerc in your home directory, which contains many settings that you may want to change. For example, you can specify the order in which messages are sorted in the index window and the name of the directory in which your folders are kept. The file is a simple text file with lots of comments that you can edit.

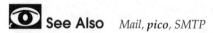 **See Also** *Mail,* **pico,** *SMTP*

PING

In the early days of the Internet, it was sometimes important to know whether or not a particular system was on-line. The command to check on a system's status is **ping**. Today, there is much less of a need to know a system's status since there is more reliability built into the Internet's structure, so this command is rarely used.

POINT OF PRESENCE

As more people want to get on the Internet, many providers have set up systems throughout the country. Because high-speed networks are much less expensive to run than they used to be, there is often no advantage to having your Internet provider be in your same city. As long as there is a high-speed connection from where you are to the host site, a long-distance works just as well. You may be in New York and your Internet provider's computer may be in California, and the distance would be invisible to you as long as there was a local phone number for you to call.

A point of presence is a bank of modems in a city that is connected through a high-speed connection to the site of the host computer that is connected to the Internet. To the users in that city, the Internet provider has a local presence, even if it is illusory. Some providers have points of presence only in nearby cities; others have points of presence across the country.

POINT-TO-POINT PROTOCOL

See PPP

POP

See Point of Presence, Post Office Protocol

PORT

When you connect to another host computer on the Internet, you need to tell it which kind of network service you want. Network services are defined by port numbers. All common network services have default port numbers; for example, Gopher uses port 70 and the World Wide Web uses port 80. Some host computers also respond to requests for communication on non-standard port numbers. For instance, a particular host computer might listen for Web requests on port 8000.

In general, you rarely need to know much about port numbers. However, if you are instructed to connect to a computer at a particular port, you need to tell your client software the number of the specified port.

POST OFFICE PROTOCOL

There are many programs that allow personal computer users to dial into a host and automatically transfer their mail to the personal computer (and transfer outgoing mail to the host). This is often better than reading the mail on the host because the software on the personal computer is more robust than the host software. Also, the personal computer mail reader can combine Internet mail with mail from other sources, such as from a local network.

In order to help facilitate this transfer, the Post Office Protocol (also known as *POP*) was developed. There are different versions of POP, and not all are compatible. Many hosts run POP servers because it is more efficient to have users reading their mail when they are not connected to the host.

PPP

In order to connect a computer using the TCP/IP communication protocol to another TCP/IP computer over a modem or a serial line, both computers must be running an additional protocol. This second protocol can be either PPP (which stands for *Point-to-Point Protocol*) or SLIP (which stands for *Serial Line IP*). Both protocols perform the same task, but they are not interoperable (that is, both ends of the connection must both be running PPP or both be running SLIP).

 **See Also**   *SLIP*

PRIVACY ENHANCED MAIL

If you are concerned with security, you need to worry about more than whether or not the files on your disk are safe from prying eyes. You also need to consider whether your communications are compromised by the low level of security on the Internet. For example, you may send mail that contains trade secrets to your colleagues; if that mail is intercepted by a competitor, you would not know it at the time.

Privacy enhanced mail, also known as *PEM*, allows you to encrypt your mail before sending it and allows the recipient to decrypt it on receipt. PEM is a proposed Internet standard for security. It uses a technology known as public key cryptography that has many benefits:

- Your message cannot be read by anyone other than the intended recipient.

- Your message is guaranteed to have come from you; no one can pretend to be you in sending the message.

- You can be sure that the entire message was sent, complete and unaltered.

For many technical reasons, PEM never really caught on. It has pretty much been replaced with other security protocols such as MOSS and S-MIME. A few minor programs use PEM, but they are difficult to find.

FOR MORE INFORMATION

Service:	**Anonymous ftp**
Host:	`ftp.tis.com`
Location:	/pub/PEM/FAQ
Description:	This file describes the proposed implementation of PEM and how to get it. It also describes mailing lists for companies that want to develop software that includes PEM.

See Also *S-MIME, Security*

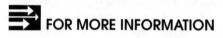

PRODIGY

Prodigy has one of the largest customer lists of any commercial network. It has dozens of useful services and has a distinctly "family" feeling to it. It has an interesting graphical interface that is both easy to learn for beginners and terribly slow.

Prodigy was the first of the large online services to give their users full access to the World Wide Web. This gave them a surge of new users, but the slowness of the service turned off many people. Still, Prodigy is still a viable option for some people who want to dabble with the Internet.

Prodigy accounts have seven digits. To send mail to someone with a Prodigy account, use that seven digit number followed by **@prodigy.com**, as in 3209123@prodigy.com.

PROJECT GUTENBERG

Getting on-line books available to everyone who wants them is the lofty goal of Project Gutenberg. The group collects and makes available books and articles that are not copyrighted. Currently, they have collected mostly older books whose copyright has run out. There are plenty of good books that fit that category. Project Gutenberg also collects some of the current literature that is not copyrighted or for which free copying has been allowed, such as the 1990 Census and some Internet guides.

 **FOR MORE INFORMATION**

Service	**WWW**
URL:	http://jg.cso.uiuc.edu/PG/welcome.html
Description:	This directory is the root for all of the Project Gutenberg archives. There are files that describe Project Gutenberg and tell you how you can participate. The files in this directory are also duplicated at many other sites on the Internet.

 **See Also** *Books, On-Line; Magazines, On-Line; Online Book Initiative*

PROSPERO

With files scattered all over the Internet, it is difficult to know how to find a particular file. Prospero is a protocol for a distributed file system that allows you to refer to remote files as if they were on your local system. This lets you be sure you have the latest versions of files on the Internet: Prospero simply makes it look like the current version of those remote files are in your directory.

FOR MORE INFORMATION

Service:	**Anonymous ftp**
Host:	`prospero.isi.edu`
Location:	/pub/prospero
Description:	This directory contains information on Prospero as well as the current version.

PUBLIC DOMAIN SOFTWARE

See archives

QUICKTIME

Using the Internet to distribute videos has always been a fascination for many people in the computer industry. Currently, the Internet is too slow and unpredictable to make this a reality, but many companies are working to change this.

One of the first successes in this process was Apple Computer's release of the QuickTime standard for video and sound playback on PCs and Macintoshes. Because the competing standards were proprietary or not very robust, QuickTime rapidly became popular. You can get programs that play QuickTime movies and sound files from a variety of places on the Internet, and some Web browsers even come with QuickTime players already installed.

RARE

See TERENA

REALAUDIO

There are many ways to get sound files on the Internet. Most of these methods are not all that satisfactory, because you have to download a whole sound file before you can start listening to it. Sound files are often large, so you can waste many minutes downloading a file only to find that it is not what you want.

RealAudio is a method to let you hear sounds from the Internet as they are being transmitted. This means that instead of downloading a whole file, you can listen as it comes over the Internet. Many companies are using this technique to broadcast sound on the

Internet in much the same way that radio is broadcast. RealAudio is a proprietary format created by a company called Progressive Networks.

 **FOR MORE INFORMATION**

Service: **WWW**

URL: `http://www.realaudio.com/`

Description: Lots of information on how to hear and create RealAudio transmissions on the Internet. This is the best place to get the free RealAudio listening software.

REC.

See Usenet News

REFERENCE BOOKS

See Books, On-Line

REQUEST FOR COMMENTS

The rules for communicating on the Internet were originally not as specific as you might think. Technical people on the Internet would suggest changes to the communications protocols, new protocols, or general improvements to the Internet. These suggestions were called requests for comments, or *RFCs*.

Many RFCs became definitions of standards used on the Internet. Almost every Internet standard is now codified in an RFC. Thus, the term *request for comments* is a misnomer: RFCs are, in fact, statements of reality.

RFCs are numbered sequentially, and there are over 1900 so far. When an RFC is amended, the previous RFC becomes obsolete and a new number is issued. Dr. Jon Postel at USC is the RFC Editor. He checks the RFCs, assigns RFC numbers, and makes sure that their availability is announced.

Most RFCs are highly technical and are only of interest to network designers. Others are much more general, covering topics such as how mail is transported and how non-Roman alphabets such as Japanese are represented on the Internet.

There are two types of RFCs that also have their own numbering schemes: FYIs (which stands for "for your information") and STDs (standards). FYIs are generally informational articles or book-length writings about the Internet, while STDs are fully-accepted technical standards for Internet communication.

➤ FOR MORE INFORMATION

Service:	**Anonymous ftp**
Host:	`ds.internic.net`
Path:	`/rfc`
Description:	This directory has all the current RFCs. There is also a current index.

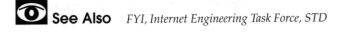 **See Also**   *FYI, Internet Engineering Task Force, STD*

RFC

See Request for Comments

RLOGIN

While you are logged into one Unix host, you may want to also log into another Unix host. The two primary commands for doing this are **rlogin** and **telnet**. Almost every system now supports **telnet**, which has become the preferred way of remotely logging in over the Internet.

RN

The most popular Usenet news reader for character-based systems is **rn**. **rn** has been around longer than other news readers and is popular with advanced readers because of features such as the ability to ignore messages on particular topics. Novice and intermediate users may find **rn**'s many features to be intimidating. Such users can easily concentrate on only those features that they need.

The documentation for **rn** is very complete. **rn** has a full-screen, character-based interface and runs on essentially all Unix computers. Almost all **rn** commands are one or two letters. **rn** commands are case-sensitive, meaning that typing **a** has a different effect than typing **A**. You can type **h** at any time to get help.

rn determines which news groups you want to read by looking in the file called ".newsrc" in your home directory. **rn** first checks to see which of the news groups listed in that file have messages that you haven't read. It then looks for news groups that are in the master list of groups that are not in your ".newsrc" file and asks if you want to add each one. Because there are often dozens of news groups added each week, you will rarely want to use this feature; it can be disabled.

You can interact with **rn** in three ways:

- You choose which news groups you want to see in *news group selection mode*

- Within each news group, you choose which articles you want to see in *article selection mode*

- As you are reading an individual article, you are in *paging mode*

After **rn** checks your .newsrc file, it puts you into news group selection mode, presenting you with the first news group in the file. If you choose to see the articles in a particular news group, you go into article selection mode for that news group. **rn** then shows you the header information for the first article; if you want to read the article, you go into paging mode for that article.

rn has some advanced features not covered here. For example, you can create a *kill file* that contains the names of subjects that you want to always skip over, or people whose postings you never want to read. **rn** also allows you to create macros that are executed each time you enter a particular news group. For more information on these and other advanced features, see the **rn** documentation.

 NOTE

If you like the interface of **rn**, but want to always see the articles grouped by subject, look into using **trn**, described in its own section. **trn** uses most of **rn**'s interface, but allows you to follow threads of ideas within a news group more easily.

Preparing Your .newsrc File

If you have run a news reader such as **rn**, **nn**, or **tin** before, skip this section. It describes how to set up your .newsrc file before running a news reader program for the first time. If you have already run either program, your .newsrc file is already set up.

One major problem with **rn** is that the first time you run it, it assumes that you want to subscribe to all the news groups in the universe. On many systems, that is over 5000 news groups, and you probably do *not* want to apply to all of them.

To fool it, you should simply create a file called .newsrc in your home directory with the names of the news groups that definitely interest you, and go from there. You can use any text editor to create this file.

Each line in your new .newsrc file should just have the name of a news group followed by a colon. For example, your file might look like this:

```
alt.health.ayurveda:
comp.simulation:
news.announce.newgroups:
news.announce.newusers:
```

The groups can be in any order: **rn** will present them in the order in the file.

How to Start rn

rn has many command line options. Normally, you will start **rn** with one option, -q, which tells **rn** not to try to add every group that is not currently listed in your .newsrc file. (When **rn** was designed, only a few new news groups were added each month, so it made sense that people would want to know which news groups were new.) For example:

```
% rn -q
```

If you want to look at just one or a few groups, you can list them on the command line as well. For example:

```
% rn -q comp.answers rec.answers
```

Another useful command line option is -S1, which forces **rn** to sort by subject the articles it shows you in article selection mode. This sorting method allows you to follow topics (sometimes called *threads*) within the news groups. For example:

```
% rn -q -S1
```

How to Select News Groups

After **rn** is finished checking your .newsrc file, you enter news group selection mode. In this mode, you are prompted for each news group that has new articles. The prompts look like this:

```
********   2 unread articles in
 comp.internet.library--read now? [ynq]
```

You actually have many more choices than **y**, **n**, and **q**. The most common commands are shown in Table 2.16.

Table 2.16: rn news group selection mode commands

Command	Description
y, Spacebar	Enter article selection mode for this news group
=	Enter select mode for this news group after displaying all the subject lines
n	Skip over this news group, going to the next group with unread articles
N	Skip over this news group, going to the next group regardless of whether it has unread articles
c	Mark all articles in this news group as read without reading them
p	Go to the previous news group with unread articles
P	Go to the previous news group regardless of whether it has unread articles
g*groupname*	Go to the named group
1	Go to the first news group

Table 2.16: rn news group selection mode commands (continued)

Command	Description
^	Go to the first news group with unread articles
$	Go to the last news group
/*text*	Go to the next news group with the text in its name (you can use wildcards in the text)
l *text*	List all news groups that have the text in their names
u	Unsubscribe from this news group
L	Show status of news groups in your .netrc file
q	Quit from **rn**
x	Quit from **rn**, not updating the .newsrc file

How to Page through Articles

When you enter a group, **rn** presents the header for each article in the order that the articles were received at your system or grouped by subject if you included the -S1 option on the command line. A typical article header looks like this:

```
Article 89276 (32 more) in
 comp.sys.ibm.pc.hardware:
From: ncdar@viewa.mudra.com (Norman Dar)
Newsgroups: comp.sys.ibm.pc.hardware
Subject: Re: CONNER Help...
Date: 22 Nov 1993 16:01:00 GMT
Organization: Mudra Systems
Lines: 37
NNTP-Posting-Host: mudra.com
Keywords: conner
--MORE--(23%)
```

You are now in paging mode, which informs you when you have more of the article to read, and tells you what percent of the article you have already read. Table 2.17 shows the commands you can use in paging mode.

Table 2.17: rn paging mode commands

Command	Description
Spacebar	Display the next page
b	Display the previous page
g*text*	Search for the text in the article
G	Search for the same text again
q	Go to the end of the article but don't mark it as read
j	Go to the end of the article and mark it as read
X	Decode and display this page using "rot13"
x	Decode and display the next page using "rot13"
Ctrl-L	Redraw the current screen
!*command*	Execute the command in a shell

When you finish reading an article, the prompt changes to something like this:

```
End of article 12 (of 15)--what next? [npq]
```

This prompt indicates that you are in article selection mode, described below.

Most of the commands in article selection mode can also be given in paging mode. In that case, rn skips to the end of the article, goes into article selection mode, and executes the command.

How to Select Articles

When you have read to the end of an article, rn puts you into article selection mode. In this mode, you have many choices, the most common of which are described in Table 2.18. These commands let you choose what article to see next, whether to save the current article on disk or to mail it to someone, whether to move on to another news group, and so on.

 **See Also** *trn, Usenet News*

Table 2.18: rn article selection mode commands

Command	Description
n, Spacebar	See next unread article
N	See next article regardless of whether it has been read
p	See previous unread article in this group
P	See previous article regardless of whether it has been read
Ctrl-N	See next article with same subject (if not in subject search mode)
Ctrl-P	See previous article with same subject (if not in subject search mode)
=	List the subjects of all unread articles
k	Mark as read all articles with the same subject as this article
c	Mark as read all unread articles in this news group
q	Go back to news group selection level
m	Mark this article as unread
u	Unsubscribe to this news group
r	Reply to the author of the article through mail
f	Create a reply to this article in the news group
F	Create a reply to this article in the news group that includes this article in the body of the new article

Table 2.18: rn article selection mode commands (continued)

Command	Description
s	Save this article into a file, using full headers
w	Save this article into a file without headers
b	See previous page of this article
Ctrl-R	Go to top of current article
/*text*	Go to the next article with the text in its subject (you can use wildcards in the text)
/*text*/h	Go to the next article with the text in its header
/*text*/a	Go to the next article with the text in the body of the article
v	Go to top of current article and display full header
X	Decode and display this page using "rot13"
Ctrl-X	Go to top of current article and decode using "rot13"
Ctrl-L	Redraw the current screen

ROT13

During more genteel days on the Internet, bawdy or otherwise objectionable Usenet news postings were often encoded with a program called **rot13**. This program made such postings unreadable to the casual viewer: you needed to run the messages through the program again to read them. This prevented those potentially offended from seeing the posting but made it easy for those who wanted to read it to do so.

Most Usenet news readers now include rot13 translation in them. On the other hand, few people bother to use rot13 and simply post the messages uncoded for all to see.

ROBOTS

One common method of indexing the World Wide Web is to have programs go out and search the Web, retrieving everything they find there. A different program collects this data, sorts through it, and make the results available to other Web users. The programs that go out on the Web are called *robots*; the collecting programs are called *search engines*. Search engines can also be used with many other kinds of databases.

ROUTER

Connecting two networks is usually easy if both networks are using the same communications protocol and you want to send all messages from one network to the other. If they don't use the same protocols and/or you don't want to send all messages between the two, it can get a bit tricky. A router, which can be hardware, software, or both, is a device that connects two networks.

For example, a router can connect a non-TCP/IP network to the Internet by converting the addresses on the non-TCP/IP side to TCP/IP addresses and vice versa. A router can also be used as a filter, rejecting data that is not intended for the network on the other side of the router, thereby reducing network traffic.

 **See Also**   *Gateway*

RX, RZ

See File Transfers

SCI.

See Usenet News

SECURITY

The Internet is inherently insecure. Data is passed unprotected throughout the network. Any host on the network can view data as it passes by without ever being detected. However, you can take steps to secure your account and files.

Security for your account and your files is always your responsibility. No one can force you to use good security measures. Account security means preventing anyone else from logging into your account; file security means preventing other people on the Internet from looking at, changing, or deleting your files without your permission.

Unix, the operating system that is used by many Internet host computers, is well-known for its high level of security. This discussion focuses on the steps you take on Unix systems. However, the concepts are often the same for other operating systems. If your Internet host uses a different operating system, be sure to ask the system administrator about how to implement security for your account.

How to Make Your Account Secure

The security for your account is based on your password. Do not give anyone your password. Someone who knows your password can log into your account and cause great harm, such as:

- Reading files that are private or personal

- Deleting or altering files without your knowledge

- Sending malicious, defaming, or slanderous mail to other people, pretending to be you

- Posting malicious, defaming, or slanderous messages on Usenet news, pretending to be you

- Changing your password so you do not have access to your own account

All of the above have happened in the past to various people who either told their passwords to others or had passwords that were easy to guess.

You use the **passwd** command to change your password on most Unix systems (some systems have commands with different names). The command first prompts you for your current password, then asks you to type a new password. It asks for the new password a second time (to be sure that you remember it and you didn't mistype it). Using the command looks like this:

```
% passwd
Old password: type your current password
New password: type the new password you want
Retype new password: type the new password
  you want again
Password changed.
%
```

It is a good practice to change your password every few months, or even more often. That way, if someone has discovered your password but not used it, you can prevent him or her from accessing your files. It is also a good practice (that is enforced at some sites) not to use easily-guessable passwords. Some common, but bad, choices for passwords include:

- Names of relatives or pets
- Numbers, such as your birthdate or the birthdate of relatives
- License plate numbers
- Your ATM password
- Names of sports, hobbies, or magazines

Check with your system administrator for more information about your company's policy on passwords.

How to Make Your Files Secure

The security for each file is based on the *permissions* you give to the file to different people. A permission tells the operating system what kind of access you want to give to that file. You can grant three kinds of permission:

Access	Meaning
Read	You can look at the file's contents
Write	You can edit the file and/or delete it
Execute	You can run the file, if it is a program

There are many files on the host computer to which you have read access but not write access; there are also many files to which you have no access.

You can grant permission to three types of people:

- the owner
- people in the owner's group
- everybody else

It is probably safe for people to ignore the "group" permissions and concentrate on the permissions given to the file's owner and to everyone else.

If your site allows anonymous **ftp** access to the system, as many do, anyone who has logged in anonymously has access to files for which the "everybody else" permissions are given. Do not assume that only people who can validly log onto your system are "everybody else."

If there are files that you do not want others to read, you want to remove the read access (and, of course, the write and execute accesses) to those files for everyone other than yourself. On the other hand, there may be files that you want others to be able to read but not modify; on those files, you want everybody to have read access but not write access. You almost always want to give yourself read and write access to all your own files.

In the example in Figure 2.29, look at the first ten columns. In the example below, look at the first ten columns:

```
% ls -l
drwx------   2 chrisr         512 Oct 28 06:39
  Bin
drwx------   2 chrisr         512 Oct 28 07:35
  Mail
-rw-r--r--   1 chrisr       40935 Oct 11 04:12
  chip-news
-rw-------   1 chrisr         230 Oct 27 13:52
  finals
drwx------   2 chrisr         512 Oct 12 20:15
  personal
-rw-------   1 chrisr      239811 Oct 29 10:22
  quick_ref
-rw-------   1 chrisr        2253 Oct 27 16:52
  temp
-rw-------   1 chrisr       10741 Oct 29 18:06
  things
```

The first column has a - if what is listed is a file, or a **d** if it is a directory. The next three letters are the permissions for the owner. In this case, all the files and directories have both read (**r**) and write (**w**) permissions for the owner. The next three letters are the permissions for the group, and the last three are the permissions for everybody else. On the **chip-news** file, note that the permissions for group and others include **r**, meaning that anyone can read that file.

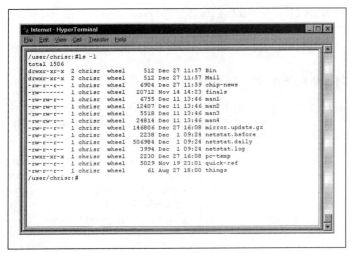

```
Internet - HyperTerminal                                    _ □ ×
File  Edit  View  Call  Transfer  Help

/user/chrisr:#ls -l
total 1506
drwxr-xr-x   2 chrisr  wheel      512 Dec 27 11:57 Bin
drwxr-xr-x   2 chrisr  wheel      512 Dec 27 11:57 Mail
-rw-r--r--   1 chrisr  wheel     6904 Dec 27 11:59 chip-news
-rw-------   1 chrisr  wheel    20712 Nov 14 14:23 finals
-rw-rw-r--   1 chrisr  wheel     6755 Dec 11 13:46 man1
-rw-rw-r--   1 chrisr  wheel    12407 Dec 11 13:46 man2
-rw-rw-r--   1 chrisr  wheel     5518 Dec 11 13:46 man3
-rw-rw-r--   1 chrisr  wheel    24814 Dec 11 13:46 man4
-rw-r--r--   1 chrisr  wheel   146806 Dec 27 16:08 mirror.update.gz
-rw-r--r--   1 chrisr  wheel     2238 Dec  1 09:24 netstat.before
-rw-r--r--   1 chrisr  wheel   506984 Dec  1 09:24 netstat.daily
-rw-r--r--   1 chrisr  wheel     3994 Dec  1 09:24 netstat.log
-rwxr-xr-x   1 chrisr  wheel     2230 Dec 27 16:08 pc-temp
-rw-r--r--   1 chrisr  wheel     5029 Nov 19 23:01 quick-ref
-rw-r--r--   1 chrisr  wheel       61 Aug 27 18:00 things
/user/chrisr:#
```

Figure 2.29: Example of the ls -l command

The **chmod** program changes the access to files. Its syntax is a bit cryptic. The first argument is how you are changing the permission, and the second argument is the file or files you are changing.

The first argument has the form *who-code-permission*. The *who* part is either **u**, **g**, **o**, or **a**, meaning **user**, **group**, **others**, and **all**, respectively. The *code* is either + or – to add or remove the permission. The *permission* is **r**, **w**, or **x** (**x** is for execute permission). You put the three together to describe how you are changing the permission.

For example, if you wanted to add read permission for others to the file called *finals*, you would use this command:

```
% chmod o+r finals
```

To later remove that read permission, you would use this command:

```
% chmod o-r finals
```

To allow others to read and write the file called *temp*, you would use this command:

```
% chmod o+rw temp
```

Note that it is probably a bad idea to give write permission to any files in your directory. There is rarely a reason to do so, and it may invite damage from malicious people.

How to Encrypt Data

Even though you may have made your files safe on your host system, sending them over the Internet is always dangerous. In order to make files unreadable to others, you have to encrypt them.

In order to be sure that data transmitted over the Internet are safe, you must use an encryption program that is so hard to break that even an adversary who knows some of the contents of the message cannot do so. Depending on your desired level of safety, such programs are widely available, both commercially and for free.

Keeping Passwords Secret

Security on the Internet goes well beyond securing the data on your computer. Almost every Internet service provider requires that you use a password in order to get access to the Internet. Further, many Web sites also require passwords in order to read the information they provide.

Keeping your passwords secret is important for many reasons. Probably the most important password is the one you use to get access to the Internet. If you tell this password to someone else, or if it is easy for other people to guess, they can use your Internet account without your knowledge. This will not only cost you money, but they can also forge email from you and no one will know that you did not send it. It is important to keep your other passwords secret for the same reasons.

One of the best ways to protect your passwords is to choose good ones, that is, passwords that other people cannot guess. For example, the names of your family members, your birthday, or names of famous people are often used, but they are also easy to guess by people who are trying to figure out the password. Much better passwords are meaningless jumbles of letters and numbers (that is, as long as you can remember them).

 **See Also** *CERT, firewalls, privacy enhanced mail, S/MIME, Unix*

SERIAL LINE IP

See SLIP

SERVER

A server is a program that performs tasks for clients in a predefined fashion. Clients and servers are described in Part 1.

SHAREWARE

See archives

SHELL

The Unix operating system has many interfaces, called *shells*, that have been written for Unix. The most common shells are line-oriented command prompts. Of these, the C shell is the most common, followed by the Bourne shell. Although the C shell is more popular, the Bourne shell is the easier of the two to use. It also has more advanced features than the C shell and can do almost everything that the C shell does. A third shell, the Korn shell, allows you to edit the command line, making it easier to correct mistakes.

If you use the Internet extensively, you will want to know some shell commands. For example, the *history* feature and its associated commands allows you to repeat a command without having to re-type it. You can also modify an earlier command without having to retype it using the history commands.

Interacting with these shells is easy. When the shell is ready for you to give it a command, it displays its *prompt*. The prompt you see differs depending on how you or your system administrator has set up your account. Your prompt may be just a percent sign:

```
%
```

Another common prompt is just a dollar sign:

```
$
```

Or, it may be your user name and a colon:

```
chrisr:
```

In fact, it can be anything, although these are the most common. In the examples in this book, a percent sign is always used.

A shell is not the commands that are available on a Unix system: the same commands are available to all shells. Instead, a shell is the way that you give the commands and see the results of commands.

SIGNATURE FILE

Many mail and Usenet news clients allow you to add text to the bottom of each of your messages. This text, commonly called a *signature*, can be decorative, humorous, or as simple as your full name and mail address. Anything that you can put in a file can be used as a signature. Note, however, that long signatures should probably be reserved for mail to good friends.

SIMPLE MAIL TRANSFER PROTOCOL

See SMTP

SLIP

In order to connect a computer using the TCP/IP communication protocol to another TCP/IP computer over a modem or a serial line, both computers must be running an additional protocol. This second protocol can be either PPP (which stands for *Point-to-Point Protocol*) or SLIP (which stands for *Serial Line IP*). Both protocols perform the same task, but they are not interoperable (that is, both ends of the connection must be running PPP or both must be running SLIP).

 **See Also** *PPP*

SMILEYS

It is often hard to infer someone's meaning when reading text they've typed, particularly if you do not know that person well. Early Internet users decided that there should be a standard way to indicate sarcasm. The symbol that was generally accepted was the smiley face:

:–)

(It helps if you look at it sideways.)

Since then, many new smiley faces (or smileys), also called *emoticons*, have been created for different purposes. None are really considered standard, and most are downright silly. Here are a few examples of smileys:

;-)   Winking

:-(Frowning

:-O   Shouting

 **See Also**   *Abbreviations*

S/MIME

Secure email has long been one of the major goals for the Internet. Unfortunately, the first two attempts at standardized secure email, PEM and MOSS, did not have much success. To get around the earlier problems, RSA Data Security invented S/MIME, a new format for secure mail.

S/MIME allows you to create any kind of email message, including those with MIME parts such as binary files, and send them securely over the Internet. S/MIME offers two types of security: encryption and authentication. An encrypted message is unreadable to anyone who does not know the secret key for the message. An authenticated message isn't encrypted, but the recipient can verify absolutely who sent them the message, thus preventing forgeries.

FOR MORE INFORMATION

Service: **WWW**

URL: `http://www.rsa.com/`

Description: This site covers all of RSA Data Security's
                    products, including their S/MIME
                    programming kits.

 **See Also**   *privacy enhanced mail, security*

SMTP

Other than the TCP/IP standard itself, the most important protocol
holding the Internet together is the *Simple Mail Transfer Protocol*,
also known as SMTP. This protocol tells each system how to form
mail messages and transfer them between computers. Together
with the standard for how to form mail headers, SMTP allows software manufacturers to create mail systems that interact completely
with Internet mail.

See Also   *Mail, Pine*

SPAM

If you were reading a newspaper, and the last paragraph of every
article was an advertisement for a product that had nothing to do
with the article, you'd probably find that pretty annoying. On the
Internet, a few people send messages to many Usenet news groups
that have no relation to the topic of the message. This is called
spamming (the derivation of the term is hotly debated by Internet
old-timers).

Spamming in Usenet or in mailing lists is considered rude and un-called for. People who spam have been widely reviled, and right-fully so. Just because something isn't illegal doesn't mean that it shouldn't be done.

 **See Also** *Etiquette*

SOC.

See Usenet News

SOURCE CODE

See archives

STD

The protocols and rules that govern the Internet are often ex-tremely technical. The main series of technical specifications for the Internet is called *Requests for Comments*, or *RFCs*. A few of the RFCs have become standards, meaning that they have been discussed and passed by organized standards groups. These RFCs were put in their own series so that they were easier to find and differentiate from proposed standards. That series is called the STDs.

The STD notes are meant to be useful to anyone who is building software or hardware that must be completely compliant with the Internet protocols. They are usually only of interest to engineers and other designers. There are over 50 STD documents.

FOR MORE INFORMATION

Service:	**Anonymous ftp**
Host:	`ds.internic.net`
Path:	/std
Description:	This directory has all the current RFCs from which the STDs are derived. There is also a current index.

See Also *FYI, Requests for Comments*

SX, SZ

See File Transfers

T-1 AND T-3

See bandwidth

TALK

You can use the **talk** command to make an Internet session resemble a telephone conversation. The **talk** command lets you type messages that appear immediately on another person's terminal. This can sometimes be useful for brief interactions; usually, mail is a better way to communicate.

To start communicating, give the **talk** command with the other person's mail address as the argument:

```
% talk lilac@pcr.com
```

The other person will see a message like this:

```
Message from TalkDaemon@buglon.com ...
talk: connection requested by
 tony@buglon.com.
talk: respond with: talk tony@buglon.com
```

To start a conversation, that person gives the command on his or her machine:

```
% talk tony@buglon.com
```

From that point on, everything you type is repeated on the other person's machine at the same time as you type it, and vice versa. To finish the conversation, press Ctrl-D.

TALK.

See Usenet News

TAR

You may occasionally find a file on the Internet in "tar" format. **tar** is a Unix utility that was originally used for putting many files at once onto magnetic tape. It is still occasionally used to batch many files into one. To unbatch a file that is stored with **tar**, use the command with the *xvf* argument, followed by the name of the file. For example, if the file you were unbatching is called *design.tar*, you would use this command:

```
% tar xvf design.tar
```

TCP/IP

The basic communication standard that holds the Internet together is called TCP/IP, which is actually two communications protocols put together. The abbreviation TCP/IP stands for *Transmission Control Protocol* over *Internet Protocol*. These two protocols, together with other agreements such as how addresses are assigned and maintained, allow computers of wildly different manufacturers and capabilities to coexist peacefully on a network as large as the Internet. If you are interested in the nuts and bolts of the protocols, there are dozens of technical books on the subject.

TELNET

A decade ago, one of the most common ways to get information from other computers on the Internet was to log onto the other computer and look at the files there. The most common method for doing this was the **telnet** command (although some people also used the **rlogin** command). There are also many graphical telnet clients for PCs and Macintoshes. Figure 2.30 shows a typical telnet client in Windows 95.

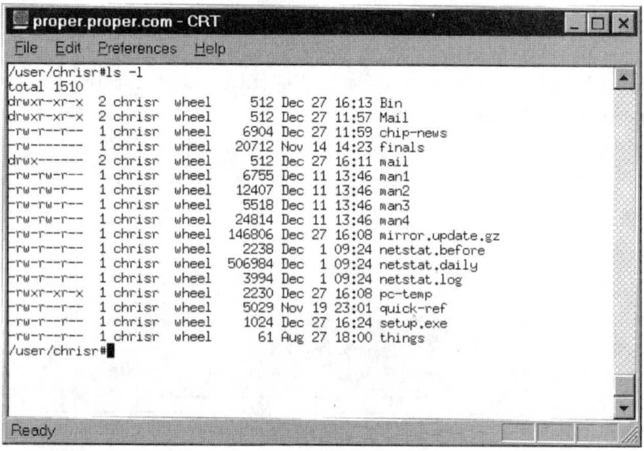

```
proper.proper.com - CRT                                    _ □ ×
File  Edit  Preferences  Help
/user/chrisr#ls -l
total 1510
drwxr-xr-x   2 chrisr   wheel       512 Dec 27 16:13 Bin
drwxr-xr-x   2 chrisr   wheel       512 Dec 27 11:57 Mail
-rw-r--r--   1 chrisr   wheel      6904 Dec 27 11:59 chip-news
-rw-------   1 chrisr   wheel     20712 Nov 14 14:23 finals
drwx------   2 chrisr   wheel       512 Dec 27 16:11 mail
-rw-rw-r--   1 chrisr   wheel      6755 Dec 11 13:46 man1
-rw-rw-r--   1 chrisr   wheel     12407 Dec 11 13:46 man2
-rw-rw-r--   1 chrisr   wheel      5518 Dec 11 13:46 man3
-rw-rw-r--   1 chrisr   wheel     24814 Dec 11 13:46 man4
-rw-r--r--   1 chrisr   wheel    146806 Dec 27 16:08 mirror.update.gz
-rw-r--r--   1 chrisr   wheel      2238 Dec  1 09:24 netstat.before
-rw-r--r--   1 chrisr   wheel    506984 Dec  1 09:24 netstat.daily
-rw-r--r--   1 chrisr   wheel      3994 Dec  1 09:24 netstat.log
-rwxr-xr-x   1 chrisr   wheel      2230 Dec 27 16:08 pc-temp
-rw-r--r--   1 chrisr   wheel      5029 Nov 19 23:01 quick-ref
-rw-r--r--   1 chrisr   wheel      1024 Dec 27 16:24 setup.exe
-rw-r--r--   1 chrisr   wheel        61 Aug 27 18:00 things
/user/chrisr#
Ready
```

Figure 2.30: Using a graphical **telnet** client

The **telnet** command is a user interface to a protocol called, not surprisingly, TELNET. The TELNET protocol must be used by both computers in order for the **telnet** program to work. Almost every Unix computer on the Internet uses the TELNET protocol, so this is rarely an issue. **telnet** has many uses on the Internet:

- Hundreds of library catalogs are available only through direct connection to the library's computers. Using **telnet** saves long-distance charges of dialing directly to those computers; some don't even allow direct dialing.

- If you have accounts on more than one computer on the Internet, you can log into the one closest to you and use **telnet** to log into the others.

- Researchers collaborating across the country can log into a single computer to run joint experiments.

There is a related program, **tn3270**, that lets you connect to IBM mainframes that expect a 3270-type terminal.

Using **telnet** is quite simple. You either start it with no arguments
or you give the name of the host on the command line. In some
cases, you are instructed to use **telnet** on a specific port; if so, include that on the command line after the host name. For example:

```
% telnet math.small.edu
Trying...
Connected to math.small.edu.
Escape character is '^]'.

Welcome to the Mathematics Department server.

login:
```

The first messages you see after you give the **telnet** command are
from the program. Once it has made contact with the remote host,
all other messages are those from the remote host. From there on,
your interactions are just like they would be if you had dialed into
the remote host.

On many systems, you will have to log in, just as you do on your
local host. Some systems, such as library catalogs, don't require
you to log in. Instead, they just start running a program, such as the
catalog interface.

When you are finished on the remote system, you should log out.
This will not always terminate **telnet**. To get to the command line
for the **telnet** program, press Ctrl-]. The prompt is **telnet>**. Only a
few of the commands, such as **quit**, are of interest to most users.
You can also use the **close** and **open** commands to end a session
with one host and start a session with another.

TERENA

Although much of this book talks about Internet work in the
United States, Europe has also been quite active in creating and
promoting the Internet. In fact, the World Wide Web was started as
part of a Swiss research project, and many significant contributions

in the standards for the Internet come from all over Europe (as well as Asia).

For many years, Europe was mostly served by two independent networks: RARE (Reseaux Associés pour la Recherche Euro-pèenne) and EARN (European Academic and Research Network). Both networks served the university and research market, which for over a decade was where most of the interest in the Internet lay.

These two networks merged in 1994 to form TERENA (Trans-European Research and Education Networking Association). TERENA is now the center for many pan-European Internet activi-ties, and is responsible for many Internet-related conferences in Europe.

 **FOR MORE INFORMATION**

Service:	**WWW**
URL:	`http://www.terena.nl/`
Description:	This site has lots of information on Internet activities in Europe, particularly at universities.

TERMINAL EMULATION

Before 1980, there were almost no "personal computers." Almost everyone who connected to a network did so on a terminal, which was essentially a keyboard and a screen that had a serial port in the back. Terminals could do little more than display characters on the screen, clear the screen, make some characters bold or highlighted, and so on.

As personal computers became popular, they began to replace ter-minals. Every computer that is to be used as a terminal, such as to dial into another computer over a modem, needs terminal emulation software. The software that you run in a personal computer to make it look like a terminal is called a *terminal emulator*.

Some software emulates many kinds of terminals, but almost every kind of emulation software emulates at least the VT100, the most popular terminal model, made by Digital Equipment. There are many freeware terminal emulation programs, and both Windows 3.1 and Windows 95 come with terminal emulators (called "Terminal" and "HyperTerminal", respectively).

TERMINAL SERVER

Many networks use high-speed lines between sites. Terminals and computers that are emulating terminals operate slowly relative to these lines, so you can combine many of them on a single line. A terminal server is a device that combines the signals of many terminals, computers, or modems into a single signal that is passed to the host computer.

TIN

The **tin** Usenet news reader represents a cross between the show-as-little-as possible approach of **nn** and show-everything approach of **rn**, two other popular news readers. **tin** reaches a happy medium by displaying all the news groups in which you are interested, regardless of whether they have new articles; it also makes it simple to see just the new articles.

Novice and intermediate users should be comfortable with **tin** (even advanced users like **tin** if they don't feel the need for the advanced feature of **rn** or **nn**). Almost all **tin** commands are one letter. **tin** commands are case-sensitive, meaning that typing **a** has a different effect than typing **A**.

Type **h** at any time to get help. When you first run **tin**, you see a mini-help window that contains the most common commands at the bottom of the screen. Once you get familiar with **tin** and want to remove that menu to free up a few more lines, type **H**.

tin determines which news groups you want to read by looking in the file called ".newsrc" in your home directory. **tin** first checks to see which of the news groups listed in that file have messages that you haven't read. It then looks for news groups that are in the master list of groups that are not in your ".newsrc" file and asks if you want to add each one. Because there are often dozens of news groups added each week, you will rarely want to use this feature; it can be disabled.

tin displays articles by subject, with replies to an article coming after the original article. A group of replies, replies to replies, and so on, is called a *thread*, because a thread of an idea runs through all of them. If you are interested in a topic, you might want to read the whole thread. If the thread is started by a question, some of the replies are probably answers. Organization by thread is the main reason that many people prefer **tin** over **rn**.

You can interact with **tin** in three ways:

- You choose which news groups you want to see in *news group selection mode*

- Within each news group, you choose which articles you want to see in *subject selection mode*

- As you are reading an individual article, you are in *paging mode*

Each of these modes has dozens of commands, the most common of which are described below.

After **tin** checks your ".newsrc" file, it puts you into news group selection mode, presenting you with all the news groups in the file; the number of unread articles in each group is marked. If you choose to see the articles in a particular news group, you go into article selection mode for that news group. **tin** then shows you a list of the subjects in that news group. You select one of the subjects to read, and **tin** shows you the first unread article in the group. You then go into paging mode for that article.

In **tin**'s menus, you can use the ↑ and ↓ keys to move up and down. You can also type **1** to go to the beginning of the menu and **$** to go to the end. Use Ctrl-U and Ctrl-D to go up and down by a page. Ctrl-L redraws the page (this feature is useful if a Unix message has appeared in the middle of a page or you had modem noise problems).

Preparing Your .newsrc File

If you have already run a news reader such as **rn**, **nn**, or **tin** before, skip this section. It describes how to set up your .newsrc file before running either program for the first time. If you have already run either program, your .newsrc file is already set up.

One major problem with **tin** is that the first time you run it, it assumes that you want to subscribe to all the news groups in the universe. On many systems, that is over 5000; clearly, this is a wrong assumption.

To fool it, you should simply create a file called .newsrc in your home directory with the names of the news groups that definitely interest you, and go from there. You can use any text editor to create this file.

Each line in your new .newsrc file should just have the name of a news group followed by a colon. For example, your file might look like this:

```
alt.health.ayurveda:
comp.simulation:
news.announce.newgroups:
news.announce.newusers:
```

The groups can be in any order: **tin** will present them in the order in the file.

How to Start tin

tin has many command line options. Normally, you will start **tin** with one option, -q, which tells **tin** not to try to add every group that is not currently listed in your .newsrc file. For example:

```
% tin -q
```

If you want to just look at one or a few groups, you can list them on the command line as well. For example:

```
% tin -q comp.answers rec.answers
```

How to Select News Groups

When you start up **tin**, you see the following:

```
Reading news active file...
Reading attributes file...
Reading newsgroups file...
```

If you see messages asking if you want to subscribe to new groups, simply type **q** (and remember to use the -q command line option the next time).

tin presents you with a screen similar to Figure 2.31. The first column is the news group number, the second column is the number of unread items in that group, the third column is the name, and the fourth column is a description of the news group. If you type **H**, the menu at the bottom disappears and you see more news groups.

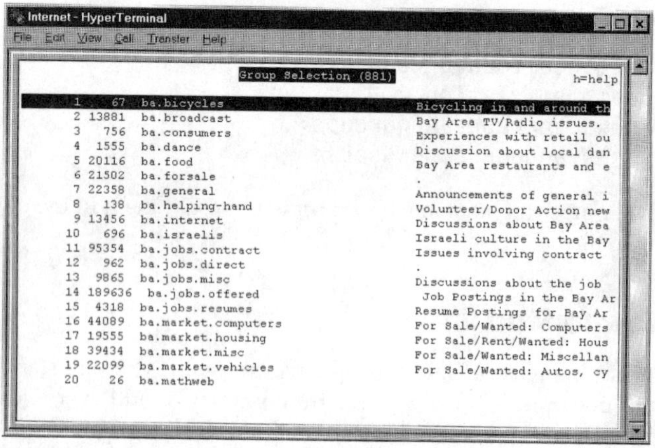

Figure 2.31: Initial **tin** screen

The commands for news group selection mode are shown in Table 2.19. You can also use the ↓ and ↑ keys to select a news group or type the number of the news group, then press ↵. To go directly to the next news group with unread articles, press Tab.

Table 2.19: tin news group selection mode commands

Command	Description
number	Select the group with that number
Enter	Read the selected group
N	Read the next group with unread articles
Tab	Read the next group with unread articles
P	Read the previous group with unread articles
p	Read the previous group
c	Mark all articles in the group as read
C	Mark all articles in the group as read and go to next group
z	Mark all articles in the selected group as unread
r	Toggle between showing all groups and only groups with unread articles
w	Post an article to the selected group
u	Unsubscribe to selected group
g	Select a named group
/	Search for a group by name
M	Change **tin** options (this works at all levels of menus)
q	Quit from **tin**
!	Run Unix shell (this works at all levels of menus)

How to Select Threads to Read

After you have chosen a news group, **tin** shows you a screen listing all the unread articles, grouped by subject.

The entries with a + after the thread number have unread messages in them. Those with numbers between the thread number and the name have responses. In this example, thread #52, **Monitor Problem**, has three responses, and at least one of those is unread.

The most common commands you can use when selecting threads are shown in Table 2.20. You can also use the ↓ and ↑ keys to select a thread or type the number of the thread, then press ↵. To go directly to the next unread article, press Tab.

How to Page through Articles

As you are reading each article, **tin** shows you information about the article at the top of the screen. When **tin** pauses at the end of a page or at the end of an article, you can choose what to do with that article using **tin** paging mode commands, shown in Table 2.21.

 **See Also** *Usenet News*

TN3270

See **telnet**

TRN

Most Usenet news groups are like rooms in which many discussions are going on at once. Some discussions are single statements

Table 2.20: **tin** thread selection mode commands

Command	Description
number	Select the thread with that number
↵	Read the selected thread
N, Tab	Read the next unread article
P	Read the previous unread article
p	Read the previous article
K	Mark all articles in the thread as read
C	Mark all articles in the thread as read and go to next thread
z	Mark all articles in the whole news group as unread
l	Create a list of all messages in the thread, showing authors; you can then select articles to read from this sub-mode
u	Toggle between showing all articles in thread groups
t	Tag the item for later mailing or saving together
m	Mail the selected article, thread, or set of tagged items to someone
s	Save the selected article, thread, or set of tagged items to a file
w	Post a new article to this news group
x	Cross-post the selected article, thread, or set of tagged items to another news group
g	Select a named group
/	Search for a subject
a	Search for an author
q	Go back to news group selection mode
Q	Quit from **tin**

Table 2.21: tin paging mode commands

Command	Description
number	Select the response within this thread with that number; 0 is the base of the thread
N, Tab	Read the next unread article
P	Read the previous unread article
p	Read the previous article
K	Mark all articles in the thread as read and read next unread article
C	Mark all articles in the thread as read and go to next thread
z	Mark this article as unread
T	Tag the item for later mailing or saving together
m	Mail the selected article, thread, or set of tagged items to someone
r	Reply to the poster of this article by mail
f	Post a follow-up to this article in the news group
s	Save the selected article, thread, or set of tagged items to a file
w	Post a new article to this news group
x	Cross-post the selected article, thread, or set of tagged items to another news group
/	Search for text in the article
q	Go back to thread selection mode
Q	Quit from **tin**

that are never replied to, but most others have replies, replies to replies, and so on. A group of replies, replies to replies, and so on, is called a *thread*, because a thread of an idea runs through all of them. If you are interested in a topic, you might want to read the whole thread. If a thread is started by a question, some of the replies are probably answers.

trn is a Usenet news reader that displays messages organized by threads. Many people find this organization method easier to follow than organization by date. As it displays each message, **trn** also shows you where in the thread to find the message.

Using **trn** is almost identical to using **rn**. In fact, each program is based on the same source code. See the entry for "**rn**" for a description of it and its commands. Here, I will discuss only the differences between **trn** and **rn**. If you are familiar with both **rn** and **nn**, you will find that **trn** is like a combination of the two.

trn has an additional mode, *thread selection mode*, that you invoke from the news group selection level by typing + instead of **y** to enter the news group. When you do, you see a screen like that in Figure 2.32. Note that each thread has one line with the name of the thread; the number on that line tells you how many unread messages there are in each thread. Each additional line below that tells the names of who has submitted replies.

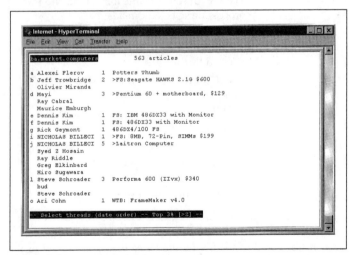

Figure 2.32: trn thread selection mode

You can select threads immediately or choose to see them only after you have processed the whole news group. The commands that you can use in thread selection mode are shown in Table 2.22.

Table 2.22: trn thread selection mode commands

Command	Description
letter	Selects the thread for processing later
y	Toggle the selection of the current thread
n	Move to next thread
p	Move to previous thread
>	Move to next page
<	Move to previous page
$	Move to last page
^	Move to first page
↵	Starts processing the current thread now
Z	Start processing the selected threads (if no threads are selected, all are processed)
X	Mark all unselected threads as read and start processing selected threads
D	Mark all unselected articles on the current page as read and begin processing any selected threads
/*text*	Search for threads with the text in their subject
L	Cycle between thread display modes (long, medium, short)
N	Go to next news group with unread news
P	Go to previous news group with unread news
q	Quit from this news group

To select a thread to read, type the letter that is at the left of the thread's line. This displays a + next to the letter. Use **n** and **p** to move down and up in the list on a page (you cannot use ↓ or ↑), and use < and > to see pages before and after the current page. To see the selected group immediately, simply press ↵.

When you are viewing articles, the commands are the same as in **rn** but the display is somewhat different. The top few lines show a map of the thread, with the current article highlighted in the map. For example:

```
(  )+-(  )--[1]+-[1]
     ¦            \-[1]
   \-[1]+-[1]
        \-[1]
```

The empty **()** at the left of the map is the root of the thread (empty parentheses indicate parts of the thread that are no longer available on your system). That message had two responses, which are the two messages in the next column to the right (the first of the two responses is also not available here). The first response had two responses, the first of which is highlighted: that is the response you are reading.

 **See Also**   *rn, Usenet News*

UNCOMPRESS

See **compress**

UPLOADING

See File Transfers

U.S. GOVERNMENT DOCUMENTS

There is a general perception that the U.S. government has not made much available on the Internet. However, there are thousands of documents available for downloading. Many are of interest to only a few people, such as scientific data, but others have very broad relevance, such as census data, policy statements, library of congress information, and so on. Recently, some states have also been making more information available over the Internet, but that is still fairly rare.

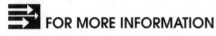 **FOR MORE INFORMATION**

Service: **WWW**

URL: `http://www.fedworld.gov`

Description: This is by far the best place to start when looking for U.S. government information and documents. It has a list of subject categories, information on all types of Internet sites supported by different branches of the U.S. government, and much more. It is sponsored by the National Technical Information Service (NTIS).

UNIX

The description in this section assumes that you know a bit about using non-Unix computers, such as what a command, a file, and a directory are. If these concepts are not familiar to you, you should probably read a beginner's computer guide before trying to do much with the Internet such as *Understnding UNIX* (also by SY-BEX). The following is just the bare minimum you should know; Unix is a very rich and complex operating system, and the following short section does not even begin to scratch its surface.

This section assumes that you are using either the Bourne or C shell. If you are using some other interface for Unix, such as XWindows, the commands described in this section may only be available to you in a C shell window.

How to Give Commands

To give a command, you simply type the name of the command, plus anything else needed by the command. For instance, to give the **gopher** command, you would type the following:

```
% gopher
```

(As described in the introduction, you only type what is in boldface characters; the other, non-boldface text on the line is already on the screen.)

How to Use Unix Directories and Files

Each account on a Unix system has a *home directory*, the place where you start out when you first log in. The home directory often is a directory with the same name as the account. It is a subdirectory of a higher directory that has some or all of the computer's home directories on it.

For example, the directory that "chrisr" starts in when she logs in might be /u12/chrisr. This means that her home directory, "chrisr" is a subdirectory to "/u12. If you are on a large Unix system, there may be many superior directories (often called "u1", "u2", and so on).

Directories and subdirectories follow the tree and branch examples you saw earlier. Figure 2.33 shows part of a typical tree of directories. The bottom of the tree is the *root directory*, called "/". The next level up has other directories called "bin", "etc", "u1", and so on.

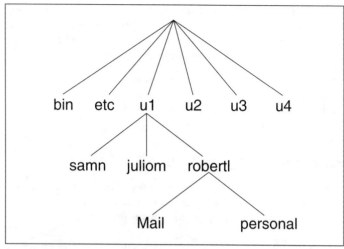

Figure 2.33: Directories and subdirectories

Your *current* directory is the one that you are in when you give a command. When you log in, your current directory is almost always your home directory.

Your home directory may have subdirectories already defined. For instance, it is common to have a "Mail" subdirectory defined. When you use the name of a directory that is under your current directory, you just use its name without the current directory at the beginning. Thus, the "Mail" directory for Chris would be called "Mail" when the current directory is "chrisr". On Unix systems, capitalization is important. In this case, note that the name of the directory is "Mail", not "mail".

You can change to a new directory with the **cd** command. For example, if Chris were in her home directory and wanted to change to the subdirectory called "Mail", she would give this command:

```
% cd Mail
```

To change to the directory that is above the current directory in the tree, use this command:

```
% cd ..
```

The .. is the Unix shorthand for "the directory that is superior to the current directory."

You can also change to a directory by giving its full name. For instance, if there were a directory called "/usr/bin" on your system, you could change to it with this command:

```
% cd /usr/bin
```

To create a new directory, use the **mkdir** command followed by the name of the directory you want to create. To make a new subdirectory called "personal" in the current directory, you would give the command:

```
% mkdir personal
```

To remove a directory, use the **rmdir** command.

Each directory can hold an almost unlimited number of files. Unix file names can be very long (usually over 100 characters), and can contain many special characters such as punctuation. However, for simplicity, you should probably restrict your file names to a reasonable number of characters (fewer than 20) and not use punctuation other than periods (.), hyphens (-), and underscores (_).

Use the **ls** command to see a list of all the files in a directory. For example:

```
% ls
Bin             finals          temp
Mail            personal        things
chip-news       quick_ref
```

The **ls** command has many possible arguments.

You can tell **ls** which files you want to see by entering a name after the command. You can use the standard * and ? wildcard characters in the name. For example:

```
% ls t*
temp            things
```

You can also use **ls** to get a list of the files in another directory. Simply use that directory's name as the argument. For instance, to list the files in the "Mail" directory, you would use this command:

```
% ls Mail
arthur              janet                  mendez
```

Another common argument is *-a*, which tells **ls** to list all information for the files.

The characters at the left of each line tell you the security permissions for each file, as described in the "Security" entry. Each line also has the name of the person who created the file, the number of characters in the file, the date and time the file was last changed, and the file name.

How to View Text Files

There are three basic methods for viewing text files:

- Type the whole file with the **cat** command

- View the file page-by-page with the **more** command

- Browse up and down in the file with an editor

In choosing your method, you should take into account the length of the file and whether you want to go back and forth or just read it from top to bottom.

To type an entire file, use the **cat** command followed by the file's name. For example:

```
% cat things
--Look for Usenet group on bicycling
--Get on insurance mailing list
. . .
```

The **more** command is usually more useful than the **cat** command because it pauses every 24 lines (one full screen) and waits for you to press a key before continuing. When it pauses you have a few choices of what to press:

Key	Action
Space	Shows the next full screen of text
Return	Shows the next line of text
/	Searches forwards for particular text
h	Shows help for the more command
q	Stops showing the file and returns to Unix

There are other commands that let you scroll forward and backward as well.

If you want to move up and down in a file, using your favorite editor is probably the best method. However, most Unix systems have only one editor, **vi**, available, and few people would call **vi** an easy-to-use editor. Check whether your system has full-screen editors such as **emacs**, **ee**, **joe**, and **pico** available, and consider using one of those instead.

How to Maintain Files

The basic commands for copying, moving, and deleting files are **cp**, **mv**, and **rm**, respectively. These commands can also be used with wildcard characters to act on a group of files.

The arguments to the **cp** command are the name of the file you want to copy and the destination. The destination can be a name of a file that does not exist, or it can be the name of a directory to which you want to copy the file. For example, to copy the file called "things" to the directory called "personal", give this command:

```
% cp things personal
```

The **mv** command also takes the same two arguments: the name of the file and the destination. If the destination does not exist, the **mv** command renames the file to the new name; if the destination exists and is a directory, the mv command moves the file to that directory. For example, to move the file called "temp" to the "personal" directory, use this command:

```
% mv temp personal
```

The **rm** command deletes files. Very few Unix systems have an *undelete* feature, so be very careful with the **rm** command. To remove the file called "temp", you would use this command:

```
% rm temp
```

How to Use On-Line Help

If you want to use Unix more extensively, you will need many more commands than those listed here. There are many good books on Unix available. Also, there is a great deal of documentation on-line on most Unix systems. The standard way to see that documentation is with the **man** command.

For example, to see all the arguments to the **ls** command, you would give this command:

```
% man ls
```

The **man** command puts out its information through the **more** command, so you can see the text a page at a time.

 **See Also** *Security*

UNIX ARCHIVES

Because Unix was almost the only operating system used on the Internet for many years (and is still probably the most used), there is no single central location where Unix utilities appear.

➡️ FOR MORE INFORMATION

Service:	**Usenet News**
Group:	`comp.sources.unix`
Description:	Although there isn't one central location for all Unix freeware, this news group is the best place to start. There are many sites that keep archives of the news group as well.

UNPACK

See **pack**

URL

The way you indicate where you are going on the World Wide Web is with URLs (Uniform Resource Locators). URLs are similar to postal addresses or telephone numbers: you use them to identify the end point of what you want.

Most URLs consist of three parts: the service name, the host name, and the request. For example, a typical URL looks like:

```
http://www.neosoft.com/internet/paml/
```

In this URL, "http:" is the service name, "www.neosoft.com" is the host name, and "/internet/paml/" is the request. It is common to have URLs where the request is just a single "/".

The most common service names you see in URLs are "http:", "gopher:", "ftp:", and "news:". These refer to Web servers, Gopher servers, FTP servers, and Usenet news servers, respectively.

A few URLs do not have a host name. The only ones of this type that you normally see are `mailto:` URLs that give an email address such as: `mailto:chrisr@english.small.edu`.

USENET NEWS

After mail, the most popular feature of the Internet is Usenet news. Usenet news is a system where messages about any subject can be posted, and other people on the Internet can reply to them. You can find discussions about politics, computer systems, religion, almost every profession, how-to's for almost anything, music, recreation, science, and so on. All told, there are more than 5000 active news groups.

To get access to Usenet news, you must have a news reader, a piece of software that knows how to read the huge database of messages and present them to you in a manageable fashion. There are dozens of news readers, and new ones are written all the time. Popular Web clients like Netscape and Mosaic come with news readers in them. For example, Figure 2.34 shows the news reader built into Mosaic. The common news readers on Unix systems are **nn**, **rn**, **tin**, and **trn**.

Each *news group* (sometimes called a *newsgroup* as a single word) is about one area. For example, the group "comp.simulation" is about computer simulation. Usenet news group names are formed in a hierarchical fashion. At the top of the hierarchy, there are names like "comp." (computers), "rec." (recreation), "sci." (science), "talk." (general gabbing and debating) and so on. There are also regional hierarchies; for example, the "jp" hierarchy is about Japan.

Many news groups have just two levels of hierarchy, such as "rec.bicycles", in which general topics of bicycling are discussed.

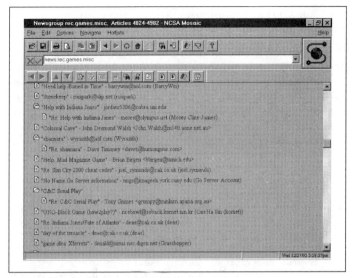

Figure 2.34: Mosaic's news reader

Other news groups can have three or more levels, such as "rec.bicy-cles.racing", where only bicycle racing is discussed.

One hierarchy of groups deserves special attention. The "alt." hierarchy is a free-for-all. In the other hierarchies, you cannot simply start a new group whenever you feel like it; in the "alt." hierarchy, you can. Thus, many of the topics in the "alt." hierarchy have a distinctly less serious tone as those in other hierarchies. Some sites do not carry some or all of the news groups in the "alt." hierarchy.

Most Usenet news groups allow anyone to post whatever they want. Often, this does not pose a problem. Sometimes, however, individuals or groups post messages that you may find annoying, upsetting, disgusting, or threatening. The decorum (or severe lack thereof) in some groups can be upsetting even to the most open-minded person. This is particularly true in some of the groups in the "alt." hierarchy. On the other hand, these groups are very attractive to other people for the freedom that they offer.

Finding which news groups are interesting to you can be difficult. The best method is to ask others with the same interests what they read. You also have some other options, besides searching through the list of all available news groups.

If you are completely new to Usenet news and don't know where to start, consider subscribing to the "news.announce.newusers" group. This is a moderated group that has useful information for people just starting out. You can't post to this group, but reading the information there is often helpful. You should also consider subscribing to local groups of interest. Almost every major city or region has local groups with both social and business discussions.

Another interesting set of groups that you should consider reading is the groups whose names end in ".answers", such as "comp.answers". These groups are moderated repositories for the *frequently-asked questions* documents (*FAQs*) generated in the groups in their hierarchy. Skimming through the ".answers" groups may give you ideas about which other news groups would interest you.

You may find that there is no group that covers your interests. You can start your own news group, although this is not necessarily easy. There is a good document that is periodically posted in the "news.announce.newusers" news group about the steps to create your own news group.

 See Also   *Frequently Asked Questions,* **nn**, **rn**, **tin**, **trn**

UUCP

During the first growth spurt of the Internet, many systems wanted to be "connected," but only once or twice a day. The idea was that they would log in, get all the mail for the people on their system, maybe get all the Usenet news, then log off. This kept phone bills down and allowed many computers that did not use the TCP/IP protocol to participate in the Internet.

In order to make this happen most effectively, many computers used the **uucp** program. **uucp** (which stands for *Unix to Unix copy*) is a program that can copy files from one Unix system to another when the two computers are connected by modem. It is fairly difficult to learn to set up, but works reasonably well once a connection is made.

uucp is still used widely today for the same reasons. Even though TCP/IP is available for almost every type of computer, many prefer to use **uucp** because they have been doing so for many years. As the SLIP and PPP protocols become more popular, it is likely that **uucp** will fade away.

UUENCODE AND UUDECODE

Most popular mail programs on the Internet cannot send binary information, only ASCII text. Thus, if you want to mail a binary file to someone, you must first convert it to ASCII. The **uuencode** program does this, and the **uudecode** program converts the file back to its binary form.

A file converted with **uuencode** is about 35% longer than the original file. In general, it is a good idea to compress the original binary file before converting it to ASCII in order to save space.

To convert a binary file to an ASCII file, use the **uuencode** command. You must supply a file label that will appear at the beginning of the file. For most purposes, you will also specify the original file preceded with < and the output file (which must have a different name) preceded with a >.

For example, to convert the file called "model" to an ASCII file called "model.uue", you would give this command:

```
% uuencode model < run-model > model.uue
```

The first argument on the command line is the line label, the next is the input to **uuencode**, and the third is the output.

You can see that the resulting file is indeed an ASCII file. The top of an encoded file looks something like this:

```
begin 600 run-model
M07EU<G9E9&$$@4F5S;W5R8V4@1W55I9&4*27-S=64@(S,@@*$
 9E8G)U87)Y(#$Y
M.3,,I"@I!==F%I;&%%B;&4@9G)E90IF;W(@82!S96QQF+6%%D9'
 )E<W-E IS=&%M
```

To decode such a file, use the **uudecode** command:

```
% uudecode run-model.uue
```

It is OK if there is some text in the file above the encoded part; **uudecode** ignores everything until the line that starts "begin."

VERONICA

There are many hundreds of Gopher servers on the Internet. In order to find which one has information that you want, you can search them using **veronica**. The Veronica database has the headings from virtually every Gopher server on the Internet and is very easy to use.

You must be running a Gopher client in order to use **veronica**. Use your Gopher client to connect to a Veronica server as described below. When prompted, enter the words you are searching for. The response is a Gopher menu of up to the first 200 titles that matched your request.

You can search for just one word, such as *chemistry*, but that will probably yield too many results to be useful. If you search for more than one word, **veronica** returns only those entries that have both words in them. For example, if you wanted to find all the Gopher menus with both the words *bioinorganic* and *chemistry*, you would enter the following:

```
bioinorganic chemistry
```

You could also put the word *and* between the two:

```
bioinorganic and chemistry
```

veronica searches always ignore the case of the letters in what you are searching for.

You can add modifiers to your search request to change the way veronica searches. For instance, you can use the word *or* to have veronica return all the menus with either of the two words in them:

```
bioinorganic or inorganic
```

You can have **veronica** return more than 200 entries by entering **-m** followed by the maximum number of entries you want to see:

```
bioinorganic chemistry -m500
```

⇒ FOR MORE INFORMATION

Service:	**Gopher**
Host:	`veronica.scs.unr.edu`
Path:	veronica
Description:	This host lets you choose from all the known Veronica database servers. It also has the latest guide to using **veronica**.

 **See Also**   *gopher*

VI

The **vi** text editor is available on almost every Unix system on the Internet. It is not nearly as easy to use as other text editors like **ee**, **joe**, and **pico**, but it has been around a lot longer and is therefore known by more people. The **vi** text editor is good for editing and viewing files; for more complex operations, you are probably better off learning a different editor.

You can either start **vi** with no arguments or the name of the file you want to edit. When you first start **vi**, you are in *command mode*, where the keystrokes you give are interpreted as editing commands. In command mode you can do the following:

• switch to *insert mode* to enter text

• move the cursor

• edit the file

• perform file actions such as saving

This section gives only an overview of the most common **vi** actions. There are many more commands available.

How to Insert Text

To insert text, you must switch from command mode into insert mode. Use one of the following commands to start inserting text:

Key	Insert Starting At
i	Before the cursor
a	After the cursor
I	At the beginning of the line
A	At the end of the line
o	On a new line below the current line
O	On a new line above the current line

When you are finished inserting text, press the Esc key to switch back to command mode.

How to Move in the File

To move the cursor, use the following keys:

Key	Movement
↑, k	Up one line
↓, j	Down one line
←, h	Left one character
→, l	Right one character
b	Left one word
w	Right one word
0	Beginning of line
$	End of line
Ctrl-B	Back one screen
Ctrl-F	Forward one screen
/*text*	Search for the text
n	Repeat previous search

You can repeat movement commands a specific number of times by typing that number before the command. For example, to go down five lines, type **5** followed by **j**.

How to Edit the File

Deleting text is easy: use the **d** command followed by a letter that describes what you want to delete. These are your choices:

Command	What is deleted
dw	Word to the right
db	Word to the left

Command	What is deleted
d0	To the beginning of the line
d$, D	To the end of the line
dd	The current line
d/*text*	To the first instance of the text
dG	To the end of the file
x	Delete the character under the cursor
X	Delete the character before the cursor

You can also use repetition with the deletion commands. For example, to delete the next five lines, type **5** followed by **dd**.

Changing is like deleting followed by an insertion command. Instead of the **d** command, use the **c** command. The only difference between the two sets is that to change the current line, you use **cd**. When you are finished inserting with the **change** command, press Esc.

How to Save the File and Quit

When you are finished editing the file and want to quit, use the **ZZ** command (**:x** does the same thing). To simply write the file to disk without quitting, use the **:w** command. If you want to edit another file after writing out changes to the current one, use the **:e** command followed by the name of the file you want to edit.

If you haven't made any changes and want to quit, use **:q**. If you have made changes and you want to abandon them, use the **:q!** command.

VRML

Computer manufacturers have long hoped to be able to make computers seem so life-like that people would think that the pictures that they see on the screen were real. The general term for this illusion is *virtual reality*, and the way that virtual reality will most likely come to the Internet is through a programming language called VRML, or Virtual Reality Modeling Language.

VRML is a way to extend other programming languages to include standard virtual reality items such as three-dimensional shapes, actions, and links. Thus, you can add VRML to other popular languages, making it much more likely that we will see more VRML-based systems on the Internet in the future.

 **FOR MORE INFORMATION**

Service: **WWW**

URL: `http://rosebud.sdsc.edu/vrml/`

Description: A great central resource for lots of information on VRML and people who are using it for interesting applications.

VT100

See Terminal Emulation

W3C

See World Wide Web Consortium

WAIS

There are many kinds of databases, each with a different method of requesting information. Some databases are very good at storing certain types of information, but most are not very good at storing free-form data. However, the Internet is full of very useful free-form data; in fact, the best information is in the least organized places, like Usenet news groups and FAQs.

In order to make searching Internet sources easier, many sites have standardized on one technology, WAIS (*Wide Area Information Server*), which allows people from all over the Internet to access different databases easily. WAIS uses an industry standard for requests and responses, which has made it much easier for programmers to create clients for WAIS searching.

WAIS lets you search for specific information in many databases at different locations. The result of a WAIS search is a single list of matching entries in those databases, ordered by how well the results matched your request. After you browse through the results, you can further refine your request using *relevance feedback.* You specify which articles are most relevant to your interests and the server looks for other articles that resemble the ones you specified.

There are many different clients for WAIS that have very different interfaces. No single client is more popular than others. Some are incredibly hard to use because they force you to choose from too many databases before you even start your search, while others let you start your search by looking through an index of the databases available.

Unfortunately, WAIS never became very popular on the Internet. It is used in a few places, but most Internet servers with databases use other methods that cannot interoperate with WAIS.

FOR MORE INFORMATION

Service:	**Usenet News**
Group:	`comp.infosystems.wais`
Description:	This group discusses WAIS servers and clients, as well as intelligent ways for the system to expand.

WEBCRAWLER

The WebCrawler was one of the first successful Web robots. WebCrawler's user interface is very simple (just one option), and it has quite a large database of Web links. Although not as fancy as Lycos, WebCrawler is probably easier to use and therefore of more value to beginning users.

FOR MORE INFORMATION

Service:	**WWW**
URL:	`http://webcrawler.com/`
Description:	This is one of the simplest of the Web search engines, but its database is as complete as many of its competitors.

See Also *Lycos, robots*

WEBMASTER

Every site on the World Wide Web has at least one person who put it together; often there are many people who work on a site to make it look the way that it does. Most sites want people on the Web to be able to contact one of the members of the Web team to give comments, ask questions,and so on. The contact person is called the Webmaster, even if they aren't the master of anything.

WEB SITE

The numerous HTML pages or Web pages are accessed at various *Web Sites*. The Web Site is identified by a *sitename* or *hostname*. Many organizations and companies are choosing domain names to make their web sites easily accessible. From there one can simply jump to a desired HTML page using hypertext links on the site's Home Page.

 **See Also** *Home Page, HTML, World Wide Web*

THE WELL

Long before the Internet became a popular topic of conversation, a bulletin boards system established early presences on the Internet. One of the best-known Internet-based BBSs was the WELL (Whole Earth 'Lectronic Link), a system in California that was originally affiliated with the popular *Whole Earth Review* magazine.

The WELL has always been a lively forum for discussion on a diverse range of topics. One of the reasons for the amount of intellectual activity on the WELL was its early adoption of the policy of "you own your own words", meaning that no one could resell your information without your permission, and that you are responsible for what you say. Many of the Internet's early social thinkers are still active members of the WELL.

⮕ FOR MORE INFORMATION

Service:	**WWW**
URL:	`http://www.well.com/`
Description:	The WELL lets its members post their own home pages on their main site. This is a good place to find out about what gets talked about on the WELL conferencing.

WHOIS

A whois database lists information about people and organizations. Searching such a database is easy using the **whois** command. The command takes two arguments: the name of the host on which you want to search, and the name you are looking for.

The largest database of people on the Internet is at the InterNIC Registration Services Host, located at `rs.internic.net`. This may become the central point for trying to find people in the future. Many universities also have whois servers.

For example, to search for anyone with the name "Keller," you would use the command:

```
% whois -h rs.internic.net keller
```

If you want to narrow your search with a first name, you might use:

```
% whois -h rs.internic.net 'keller, james'
```

 **See Also** *Addresses, Mail*

WIDE AREA INFORMATION SERVER

See WAIS

WINDOWS ARCHIVES

See PC Archives

WINSOCK

For many years, there was no consistent way to access TCP/IP through Microsoft Windows. Commercial vendors who grew tired of program incompatibilities worked together to create the Winsock standard. Winsock, which is short for "Windows Sockets," allows all Internet programs for Windows to work using the same connection to the Internet.

Winsock is also valuable for communications protocols other than TCP/IP. There are versions which support Novell's IPX/SPX and

DEC's DECNet. Some versions of Winsock are free, others are shareware, and others come as part of commercial software.

WORLD WIDE WEB

Just as it is difficult to give a short explanation of what the Internet is, it is also difficult to describe just what the World Wide Web is. The Web, as it is commonly known, is a set of protocols that give Internet users interactive access to a huge variety of content on the Internet. In many people's view, however, the Web is the content itself, and not the underlying protocols.

Hypertext has long been touted as the best way to unify access to a wide variety of information. The central part of the Web is a protocol, HTTP, that allows users to easily make hypertext information available to other users. For instance, you might write a document that has a brief overview of a particular topic. In that document, you could refer to another document with a more complete description of the topic, and you could make that document available to the reader. The reader could simply choose it and it would be retrieved.

There is World Wide Web client software available for all types of computers. For PCs and Macintoshes, Netscape is the most common Web client software; however, there are dozens of different programs to choose from. On character-based Unix systems, **lynx** is the most common program used to access the Web. Figure 2.35 shows Emissary from Attachmate running on Windows 95.

The World Wide Web supports many kinds of documents, such as text, formatted text, pictures, video, and sounds. One of the best features of the Web is that the kinds of information you can see on it is expanding all the time. If a software company comes up with a new type of information, they can create programs to view that information, and those programs can interact with Web clients with almost no effort on the part of the user.

The Web is much more than just hypertext, however. Most Web client software can access many different types of Internet servers.

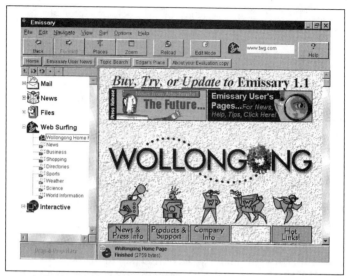

Figure 2.35: Emissary Web client

For example, Netscape can access HTTP servers, FTP servers, Gopher servers, Usenet news servers, WAIS servers, and many others as well. When popular Web clients add new kinds of servers to their repertoire, the Web grows by that much more.

Tens of thousands of people and companies have set up World Wide Web servers. Some Web sites consist of a single page about a person, while others consist of hundreds of pages of information about a company's products. Web sites can be simple, text-based pages, but many have elaborate graphics, sound, videos, and so on. For example, Figure 2.36 shows Sybex's Web site, which has information on all of their books.

Using the World Wide Web to distribute information that has references to other information helps reduce the amount of traffic on the Internet. When you access a document using a World Wide Web client, the document is transferred to your computer, but the connection is then terminated. This prevents the Web server from having to hold open a line while you read the document.

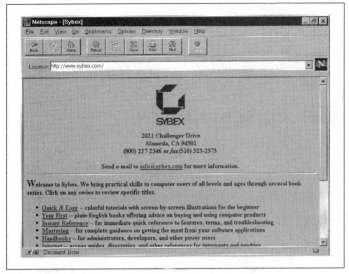

Figure 2.36: Web page for Sybex

The Web is one of the most exciting parts of the Internet, and certainly the part that is getting the most publicity right now. Although more people use email, the Web has attracted much more interest from media companies, banks, and merchants.

 **See Also**   *HTML, lynx, Mosaic, Netscape, Website, www*

WORLD WIDE WEB CONSORTIUM

The World Wide Web Consortium, better known as the W3C, is an industry group whose mission is to help further the Web by giving guidance and technical support. The W3C is based at the Massachusetts Institute of Technology, and has a permanent staff of researchers and administrators.

Because the Web is moving in many directions at once, the W3C is an important central spot for the companies and researchers working on the Web to coordinate their work. For example, the W3C is helping move forwards the standards for both HTML and HTTP. The W3C also sponsors conferences about the technical and non-technical aspects of the Web.

FOR MORE INFORMATION

Service:	**WWW**
URL:	`http://www.w3.org/`
Description:	This server has a wealth of information on the World Wide Web, with everything from beginner's guides to advanced programming tools. The site also has research reports from the W3C about where the Web is going in both the short and long terms.

WWW

One of the first clients for the World Wide Web is a line-oriented browser called **www**. **www** has mostly been replaced by **lynx** because **lynx** has an easier-to-understand user interface. However, you may want to use **www** if **lynx** is not available on your Unix host or if your terminal does not work with **lynx**.

When you start **www**, you see a screen similar to that in Figure 2.37. Notice the command line at the bottom of the screen. **www** displays a screen's worth of information and pauses.

Each of the numbers in square brackets represents a linked item. To follow a link, you type the number of the link and press ↵. To see the next page of text for the current document, press ↵ by itself. The commands that you are likely to use are shown in Table 2.23.

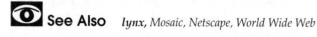 **See Also**   *lynx,* Mosaic, Netscape, World Wide Web

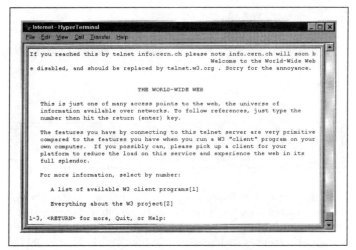

Figure 2.37: www initial screen

Table 2.23: www commands

Command	Description
Enter	View next page of the document
U	View previous page of the document
number	View the linked document with that number
BO	Go to the last page of the document
T	Return to the first page of the document
L	List the references from this document
>*file*	Save the text of this document in the file
>>file	Append the text of this document to the file
H	Get brief help
M	Read the on-line manual for **www**
Q	Quit from **www**
! *command*	Execute shell command

XMODEM

See File Transfers

XWINDOWS

While the majority of Internet users dial in through modems, a significant number are directly connected to the Internet through local area networks. Many of those people use Unix workstations with advanced graphics capabilities. During the mid-1980s, a standard for displaying graphical information on such workstations was developed. The XWindows standard allowed software and operating system designers to be able to write a single application that worked on a wide variety of graphics terminals.

The reason that XWindows is not used on most personal computers connected to the Internet through modems is that it is a very communications-intensive system. The designers of XWindows assumed that the terminal would have a very fast connection with the host system and that it was acceptable to fill up that connection with messages. While this is OK (although not great) for local area networks with a single server, it is almost unworkable over even the fastest modems.

There is a great deal of Internet software written for the XWindows standard. There are XWindows-based clients for many client/server systems such as Gopher, Usenet news, mail, and the World Wide Web.

YAHOO

What started as a small, part-time project to list the best spots on the Web has turned into one of the most popular Web starting spots. Yahoo differs from other Web sites that list Web sites in that it is not based on a robot that goes wandering around the Web. Instead, the tens of thousands of entries in its databases are all created by people who know something about the Web sites. Figure 2.38 shows some of the main headings for Yahoo's catalog.

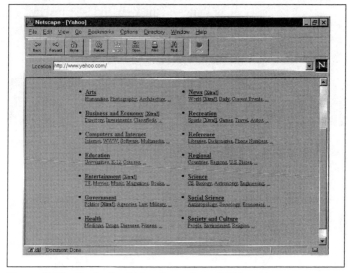

Figure 2.38: Exploring Yahoo's catalog of Web topics

Because the information is generated and cataloged by people, Yahoo is much more than a search engine. The listings are structured hierarchically, so you can see all the related sites at one time. For example, if you are looking for Internet-based information on dogs, instead of searching for the word "dog", you could go to the page that has dozens of dog-related sites and choose the ones to go to based on their descriptions.

Yahoo also allows you to search, so that you don't have to guess where something that you are interested in is cataloged. Thus, a search for the word "dog" will also turn up information about Web sites where there are photos of the site's owner and their dogs.

FOR MORE INFORMATION

Service:	**WWW**
URL:	`http://www.yahoo.com/`
Description:	This is one of the best places to look for other things on the Web, and is visited by hundreds of thousands of people every day.

YMODEM

See File Transfers

ZMODEM

See File Transfers

Index

Symbols

B

C